Historium

For Natalie and Otto
R.W.

For Brother Jo
J. N.

First U.S. edition 2015

Library of Congress Catalog Card Number 2014949929
ISBN 978-0-7636-7984-2

15 16 17 18 19 20 CCP 10 9 8 7 6 5 4 3 2 1

Printed in Shenzhen, Guangdong, China

This book was typeset in Gill Sans and Mrs Green.
The illustrations were drawn and painted digitally.

BIG PICTURE PRESS
an imprint of
Candlewick Press
99 Dover Street
Somerville, Massachusetts 02144

www.candlewick.com
www.bigpicturepress.net

Historium

illustrated by RICHARD WILKINSON

written by JO NELSON

BPP

Preface

Human beings are astonishingly creative. For over a million years, they have been innovating, making not just functional tools but elaborate objects and intricate artwork as well.

At first glance, the purpose and significance of an ancient artifact may seem unclear, but explored in its context, it becomes a window onto a distant time and place. The scratched lines on a piece of ochre may seem unremarkable until you learn that they are 70,000 years old and the earliest known example of a person making a decorative pattern. A small clay figure may look rather ordinary until you imagine it as one of thousands of tomb guardians, handcrafted to protect an immense mound where a Japanese emperor was buried.

Understanding objects in their context also enables us to make links between civilizations and recognize more general themes that emerge in human societies. A Mesopotamian board game and an ancient Egyptian model of bread makers appear to have little in common until you discover they were both chosen to accompany the deceased to the afterlife.

Writing about the objects in this museum has taken me on a tour of ancient and still-thriving cultures around the world. I've feasted with Celts, fought with Persians, traded with African kings, felt the power of rock art with Australia's Aboriginal people, built elaborate temples, and attended all kinds of ancient rituals. Now I'd like to invite you to do the same.

Jo Nelson
Author of *Historium*

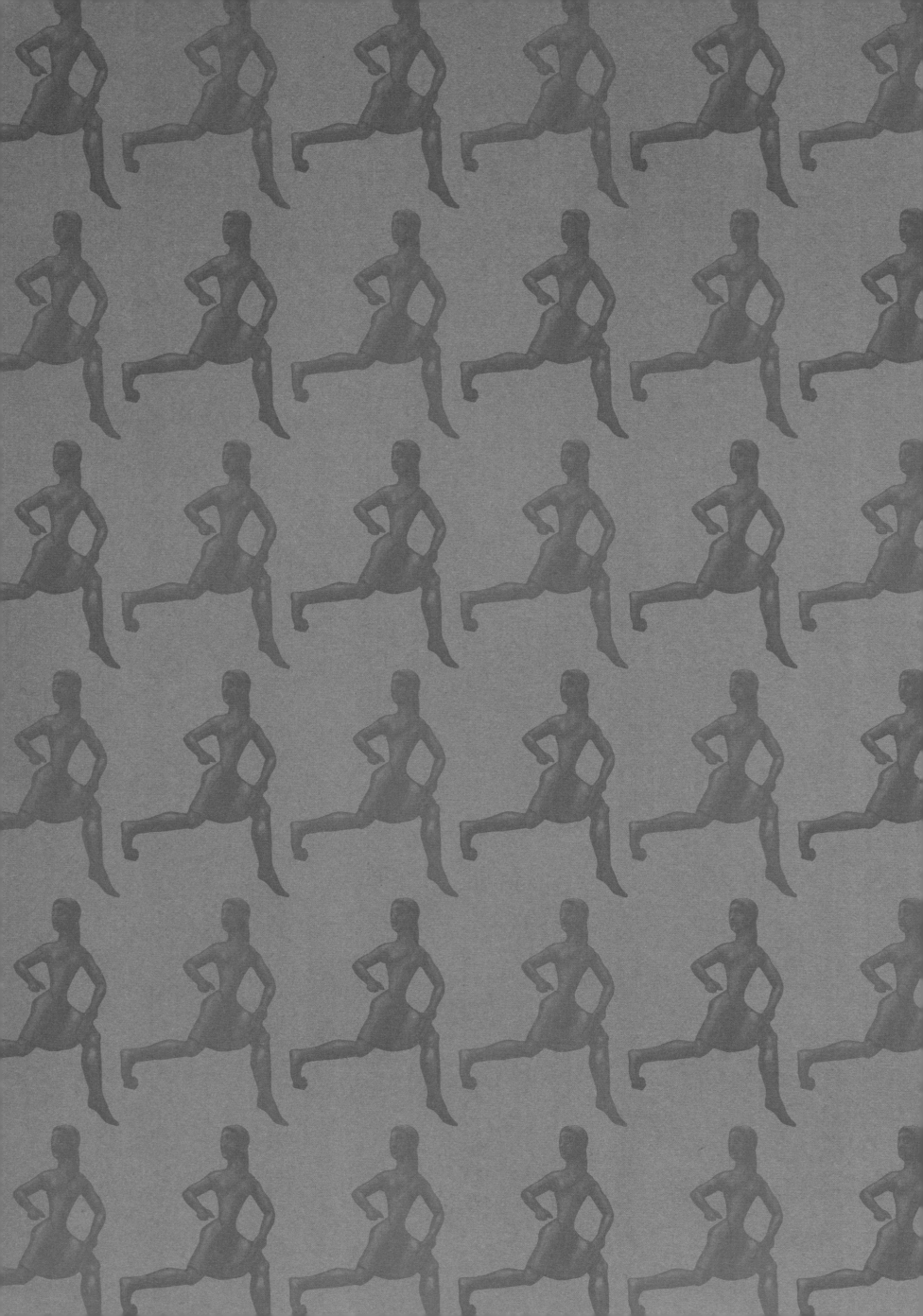

Entrance

Welcome to Historium

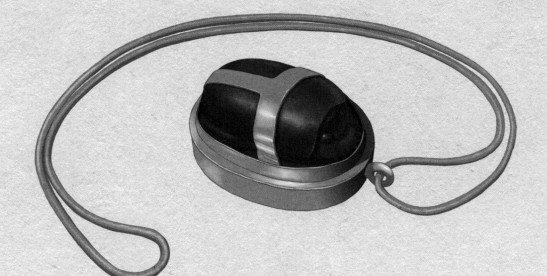

Historium's curators gave a great deal of thought to which objects we wanted to include in this museum. It would take a museum of unimaginable proportions to adequately represent the many rich and varied cultures of the past.

So first, we tried to choose a diverse and wide-ranging selection of civilizations to showcase, and second, we sought to select items that were representative of and provided telling insights into the cultures they were a part of.

We hope the offerings we've chosen will inspire future exploration. On display you will find items of ritual and religion, of death and burial, of adornment and spectacle, of writing and story, of everyday life and work, of warfare and power.

As you wander through the museum, you will be able to compare one civilization to the next. Perhaps you will notice similarities; perhaps you will notice differences. Certain names and themes will appear repeatedly, revealing some surprising connections. Your visit will be a journey not only around the world but also through time, from stone hand axes made a million years ago in Africa to tenth-century pottery made by the Pueblo people of America in a tradition that is still very much alive today. So turn the page, step back in time, and let your journey begin.

What Is Archaeology?

Archaeology is the study of the past through the traces civilizations have left behind. These traces can include a wide range of artifacts—from the earliest stone tools and the ruins of ancient settlements to burial goods and fragments of writing.

To understand the importance of archaeological objects, they must be put in context through careful detective work. Archaeologists take many samples from discovery sites for close analysis. A technique called carbon dating can roughly determine the age of any organic material, while traces of pollen can reveal the types of vegetation around at the time. Similar types of objects, such as pieces of pottery, are compared and classified to form a useful time line.

Modern archaeologists are meticulous in their research, but this has not always been the case. Early excavations were more like hunts for buried treasure than attempts to understand the past. Objects were removed and sold for their material worth rather than being valued for their cultural significance. It was only in the eighteenth and nineteenth centuries CE that scholars began to appreciate the historical importance of ancient artifacts, but even then many treasures were taken a long way from their places of origin to be displayed in museums around the world. Today there is much debate about where items now held in museum collections rightfully belong. Some ancient cultures, such as the Pueblo and the Māori, are still thriving today, and people from those cultures have sought, and continue to seek, the return of sacred and culturally important items.

Modern archaeology takes a scientific approach to learning from objects, and today, new technologies, from electron microscopy to satellite imagery, have made the discipline more accurate than ever, with each new discovery improving our understanding of the past. As you explore the different objects in *Historium*, take a moment to think what traces you and your community might leave behind: How might your cell phone, your backpack, or your toothbrush be understood several thousand years from now?

TIME LINE OF *HISTORIUM* OBJECTS

Africa

Southern Africa
Stone Age hand ax
700,000–1,000,000
years old
PAGES 8–9

Southern Africa
Blombos ochre stone
70,000 years old
PAGES 8–9

Ancient Egypt
Wall relief
from tomb of
Djehutyhotep
Around 1850 BCE
PAGE 20

Ancient Egypt
Ram's head amulet
712–664 BCE
PAGES 16–17

Ancient Egypt
Bust of Queen Nefertiti
Around 1340 BCE
PAGES 18–19

America

The Olmec
Colossal stone head
1200–900 BCE
PAGES 24–25

The Olm
Seated fe
figurine
900–500
PAGES 24–

Asia

Ancient China
Neolithic bowl
3200–2700 BCE
PAGE 44

Ancient India
Indus Valley
civilization
dancing girl
Around 2500 BCE
PAGE 40

Ancient China
Cauldron from the
tomb of Fu Hao
1300–1046 BCE
PAGE 44

Europe

Ancient Greece
Dinos (mixing bo
Seventh century
PAGE 55

The Middle East

The Ancient Levant
Copper scepter
4500–3500 BCE
PAGES 74–75

Mesopotamia
Statuette of a goat from Ur
Around 2600–2500 BCE
PAGES 68–69

Mesopotamia
The Deluge Tablet
Seventh century BCE
PAGES 72–73

Oceania

Melanesia
Lapita pottery
fragments
1000 BCE
PAGES 84–85

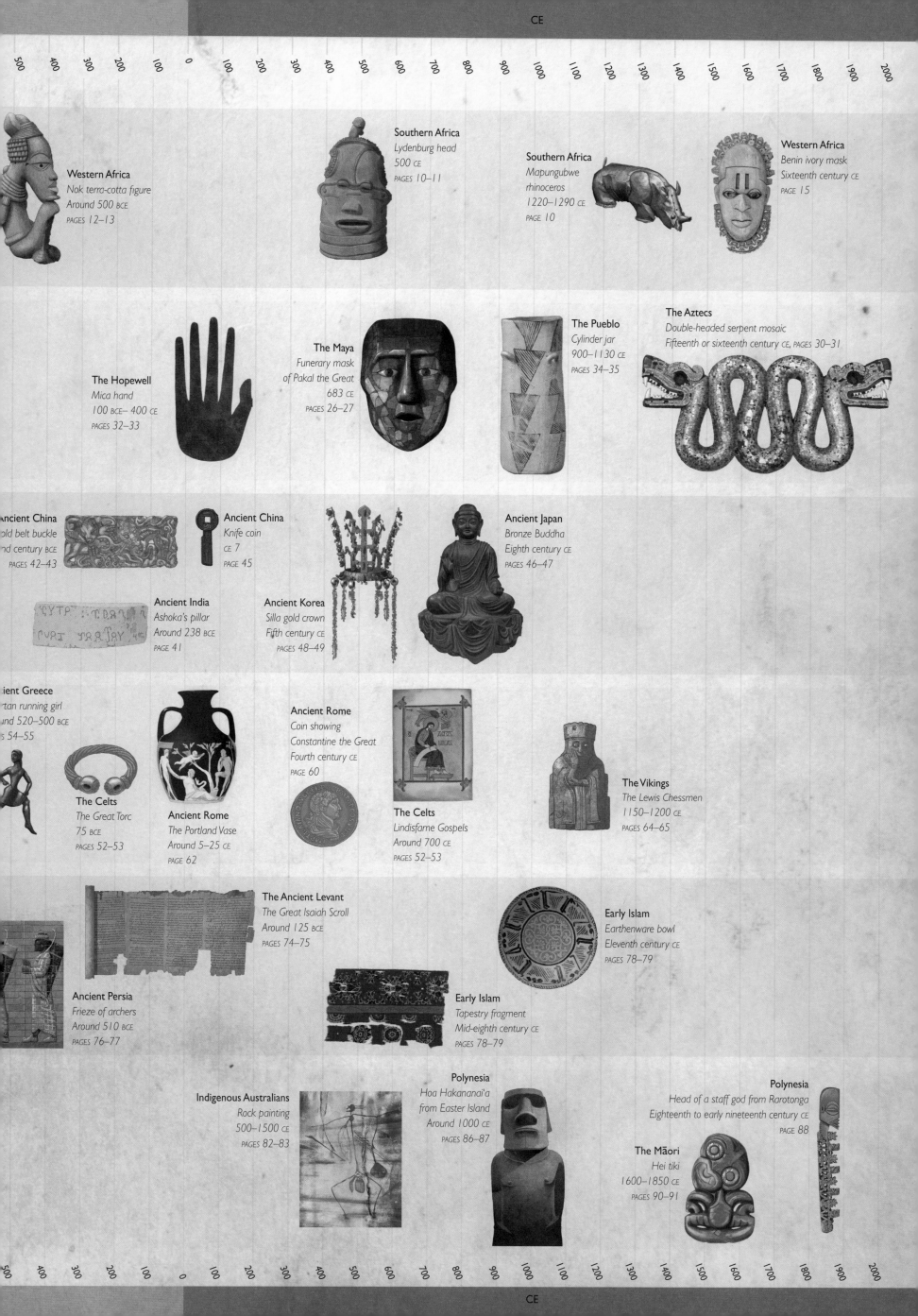

500 400 300 200 100 0 100 200 300 400 500 600 700 800 900 1000 1100 1200 1300 1400 1500 1600 1700 1800 1900 2000

Western Africa
Nok terra-cotta figure
Around 500 BCE
PAGES 12–13

Southern Africa
Lydenburg head
500 CE
PAGES 10–11

Southern Africa
Mapungubwe
rhinoceros
1220–1290 CE
PAGE 10

Western Africa
Benin ivory mask
Sixteenth century CE
PAGE 15

The Hopewell
Mica hand
100 BCE– 400 CE
PAGES 32–33

The Maya
Funerary mask
of Pakal the Great
683 CE
PAGES 26–27

The Pueblo
Cylinder jar
900–1130 CE
PAGES 34–35

The Aztecs
Double-headed serpent mosaic
Fifteenth or sixteenth century CE, PAGES 30–31

Ancient China
Gold belt buckle
Second century BCE
PAGES 42–43

Ancient China
Knife coin
CE 7
PAGE 45

Ancient Japan
Bronze Buddha
Eighth century CE
PAGES 46–47

Ancient India
Ashoka's pillar
Around 238 BCE
PAGE 41

Ancient Korea
Silla gold crown
Fifth century CE
PAGES 48–49

Ancient Greece
Spartan running girl
Around 520–500 BCE
PAGES 54–55

The Celts
The Great Torc
75 BCE
PAGES 52–53

Ancient Rome
The Portland Vase
Around 5–25 CE
PAGE 62

Ancient Rome
Coin showing
Constantine the Great
Fourth century CE
PAGE 60

The Celts
Lindisfarne Gospels
Around 700 CE
PAGES 52–53

The Vikings
The Lewis Chessmen
1150–1200 CE
PAGES 64–65

The Ancient Levant
The Great Isaiah Scroll
Around 125 BCE
PAGES 74–75

Early Islam
Earthenware bowl
Eleventh century CE
PAGES 78–79

Ancient Persia
Frieze of archers
Around 510 BCE
PAGES 76–77

Early Islam
Tapestry fragment
Mid-eighth century CE
PAGES 78–79

Indigenous Australians
Rock painting
500–1500 CE
PAGES 82–83

Polynesia
Hoa Hakananai'a
from Easter Island
Around 1000 CE
PAGES 86–87

Polynesia
Head of a staff god from Rarotonga
Eighteenth to early nineteenth century CE
PAGE 88

The Māori
Hei tiki
1600–1850 CE
PAGES 90–91

500 400 300 200 100 0 100 200 300 400 500 600 700 800 900 1000 1100 1200 1300 1400 1500 1600 1700 1800 1900 2000

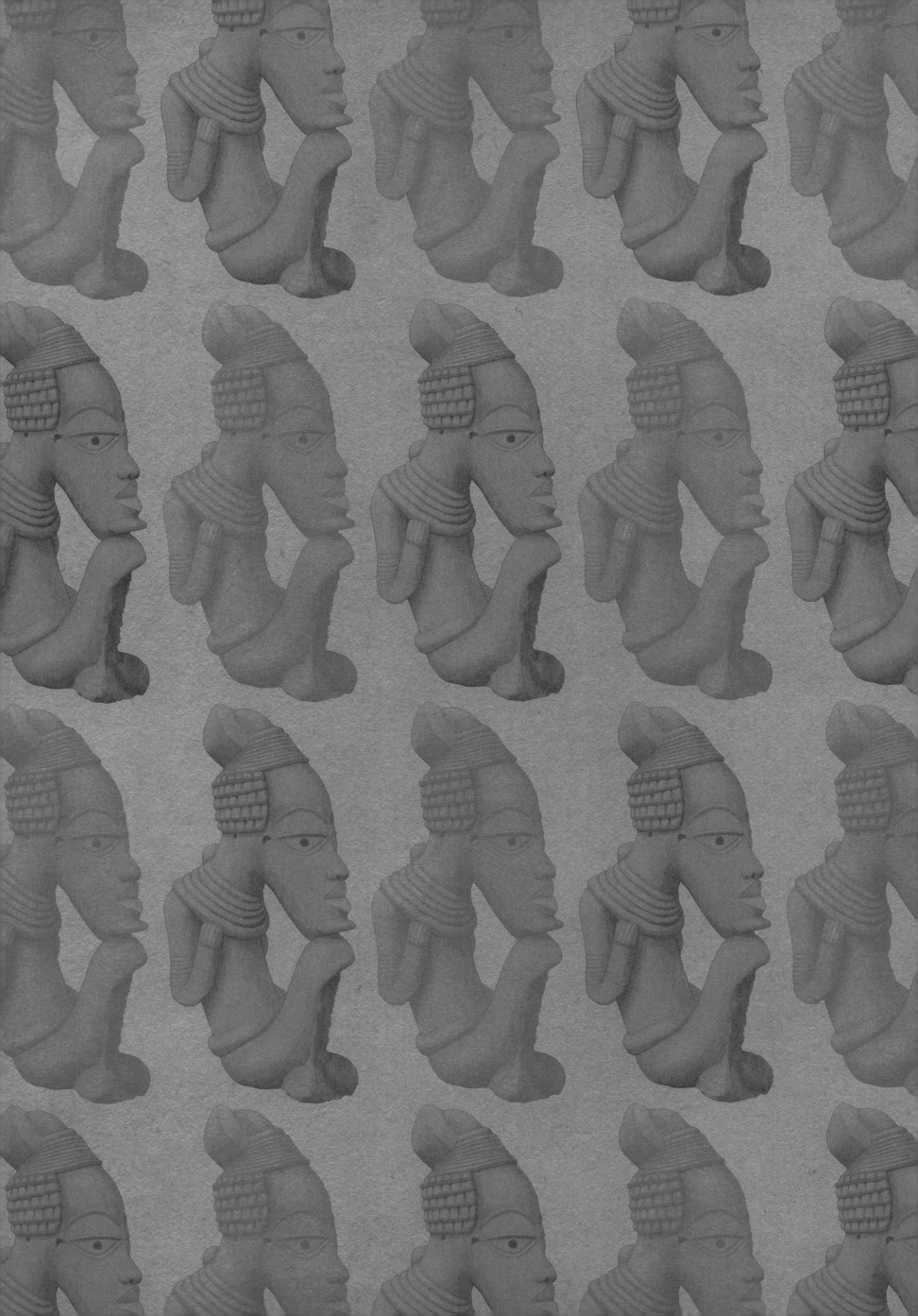

Gallery 1

Africa

Southern Africa
Western Africa
Ancient Egypt

Southern Africa

Africa has the longest record of human inhabitants of any continent in the world. The earliest stone tools were found in eastern Africa, and early human tool-makers seem to have spread to southern Africa around one million years ago. It is thought that the evolution of fully modern human beings occurred around two hundred thousand years ago, in eastern and southern Africa's savannah woodlands.

Cave paintings, shell beads, and careful burial sites give clues to the daily lives and spiritual beliefs of hunter-gatherers in the late Stone Age. Evidence of herding animals and making pottery in eastern Africa dates from around 8000 BCE, and these practices appear to have spread to southern Africa by about 500 BCE. Around 200 CE, iron-using farmers appeared, and agricultural communities quickly spread across the region.

The Limpopo and Save Rivers were used as early trade routes in southern Africa, taking ivory and gold from inland areas to trading posts on the coast. In the eleventh century CE, the first urban centers emerged in the region. The state of Mapungubwe and the Great Zimbabwe kingdom both owed their prosperity to the export of gold. Their trade networks reached to eastern Africa, Arabia, India, and even China. As these centers flourished, so did the artistic endeavors of the people.

Away from the trading centers, most people still lived in small-scale farming communities with societies based around kinship. The arrival of Portuguese mariners in the fifteenth century CE marked the beginning of European interaction with southern Africa.

Key to plate

1: Stone Age tools
700,000 to 1,000,000 years old
These hand axes were found in Kathu in northern South Africa. With sharp points at one end and sharp edges down the sides, these stones were expertly chipped and shaped to make highly versatile hand axes. The hand ax was the tool of choice for human ancestors for over a million years. Its sharp edges would have cut vegetation or meat and scraped bark or animal skins, while its point could have been used as a drill. The area of the brain used to make a tool like this overlaps with the area used for spoken language. It is highly possible, therefore, that humans from the early Stone Age already had some command of language.

2: Blombos ochre stone
Around 70,000 years old
Engraved ochre stones from the Blombos Cave are the oldest known examples of intricate designs made by humans. The geometric markings, etched with the point of a stone, are an astonishing example of very early creative behavior. The Blombos Cave contained many more lumps of ochre, which were shaped in a way that suggests they were being used for their pigment. The soft, iron-rich ochre would have been ground to a powder and turned into a reddish paint, perhaps for cave or body painting. Shell beads and bone tools found alongside the ochre stones support the idea that the early humans using this cave were interested in ornamentation.

3: The Coldstream Stone
Date unknown
This painted stone was found buried with a human skeleton near the southern coast of South Africa. The main rock artists of southern Africa were the San hunter-gatherers. The painting of three figures in red, black, and white is well preserved and unusual for its variety of colors. The figures on this burial stone may well be San medicine men performing a dance to enter the supernatural world. The central figure appears to be carrying a bow and hunting arrows over his shoulder. In his hands he carries what is thought to be a feather and a palette, suggesting that he is an artist. Most rock art is found on cave walls and depicts either animals or humans.

1

2

3

4

Key to plate

4: Mapungubwe rhinoceros
1220–1290 CE
This gold-foil rhinoceros was discovered in a royal grave at Mapungubwe, one of southern Africa's first states. The site reveals the existence of a ruling elite living separately on a hilltop settlement. This is the first known example of a class-based society in southern Africa. Among the grave goods were ceremonial artifacts made of gold, copper, ceramics, and glass beads originating from India, Egypt, and Arabia. They reveal Mapungubwe's position as a wealthy trading center, with links to cultures across the Indian Ocean. Climate change at the end of the thirteenth century brought drought and crop failure to Mapungubwe, causing the Iron Age community to disperse.

5: Gold bowl and scepter
1220–1290 CE
These gold items were also found in graves on the hill at Mapungubwe. Natural gold deposits in the area contributed to the state's wealth, and gold was a valuable trade commodity. Gold was also crafted into ornaments and jewelry for the local elite. At its height, Mapungubwe was the largest state in southern Africa.

6: Lydenburg head
Around 500 CE
This is one of seven fired earthenware heads, in a variety of sizes, found carefully buried in a pit outside the town of Lydenburg in northeastern South Africa. They date from southern Africa's early Iron Age and are the earliest known examples of sculpture in southern Africa. The heads are hollow with thin clay strips added to create facial details. It is possible the larger heads were intended as helmet masks, to be worn as part of a ceremony. The

skill and thought that went into the designs suggest that they were valued products of a well-organized and settled community.

7: Great Zimbabwe soapstone figure
Around fifteenth century CE
The ancient city of Great Zimbabwe was the heart of the thriving Shona Empire from the eleventh to the fifteenth century CE. Its wealth lay in cattle production and in gold and ivory trade. Extensive stone ruins of the impressive city with its 66-foot/20-meter wall still remain today, including eight birds carved in soapstone that once sat on walls and monoliths. It is thought they represent the bateleur eagle, a good omen, protective spirit, and messenger from the gods in Shona culture. The much smaller soapstone figure shown here is also thought to be from Great Zimbabwe. Its fascinating style recalls the famous bird columns, although its age and precise origin are unknown.

5

6

7

Western Africa

The oldest known ironworking culture in western Africa is the Nok civilization, which existed from at least 900 BCE to around 200 CE. The impressive terra-cotta statues from this time and the iron furnaces found alongside them speak of an advanced, organized society.

By around 400 BCE, ironworking was fairly widespread in western Africa. Iron tools helped farming communities spread more quickly, and some of these communities developed into large states. Copper was scarce in western Africa, so communities imported it from northern Africa or mines in the Sahara Desert. These copper routes would have also encouraged a flow of ideas and influences across the continent.

Western Africa has a long and rich oral tradition, but no indigenous writing existed until the nineteenth century CE. The earliest written accounts about the area are by Muslims from northern Africa and date from the tenth century CE. They describe large towns and cities, with markets, trade networks, and systems of government ruled by kings.

Notable civilizations among the western African states were the kingdom of Ife, the kingdom of Benin, and the Mali Empire. These states emerged from around the eleventh century CE and reached the height of their powers in the fourteenth and fifteenth centuries CE. Their prosperity was reflected in high levels of artistic achievement, including glorious brass, bronze, terra-cotta, and ivory artifacts.

--- *Key to plate* ---

8: Terra-cotta equestrian figure
Thirteenth to fifteenth century CE
The Mali Empire (eleventh to sixteenth century CE) had a well-organized army with an elite corps of horsemen and many foot soldiers in each battalion. Mali's wealth stemmed from its gold mines and its regular surplus of crops.

The army guarded the empire's borders and protected the all-important trade routes. This equestrian figure is one of hundreds of different terra-cotta sculptures made during the time of the Mali Empire. The very fact that Mali had a cavalry is evidence of the empire's prosperous economy.

Horses are not indigenous to Africa, so they would have been expensive animals to acquire and look after, not to mention the cost of bridles and other equipment. A successful empire needed a strong ruler. Unfortunately, weak rulers in the fifteenth and sixteenth centuries sent the empire into decline.

8

10

9

Key to plate

9: Seated dignitary

Around 500 BCE

This terra-cotta figure from the Nok culture (named after the village where the first terra-cotta sculpture was found) is the product of an ancient Iron Age culture. Other human heads, figures, and animals have been discovered over hundreds of square miles. They all share similar characteristics, such as the triangular, pierced eyes and elaborate hairstyling. The sculptures are hollow and built from clay coils. Their significance and purpose are unknown, but their sophisticated design and execution suggests a long tradition of terra-cotta art in the area. This figure is heavily adorned with jewelry and appears to be of high status. His crooked baton and flail are symbols of authority that may have been borrowed from ancient Egypt.

10: Ivory armlet

Fifteenth to sixteenth century CE

The ruler of the Edo people of Nigeria is called the Oba of Benin. Ivory represents his longevity, strength, wealth, and purity. The most elaborate ivory carvings are reserved for the Oba. This armlet features the Oba with mudfish legs and arms raised skyward. Since mudfish live on both land and sea, they are symbolic of the Oba having both spiritual and secular powers. The current Oba traces his origins to a dynasty that began in the fourteenth century.

11: Brass plaque

Sixteenth century CE

This brass plaque is one of more than nine hundred still in existence today, which once covered the interior walls of the Oba of Benin's royal palace in Benin City, in modern-day southern Nigeria. The plaques pay honor to the Oba by depicting his victories in battle and showcasing court rituals.

The plaque figures are set in high relief and are beautifully executed. This particular plaque includes two Europeans—the tiny attendants floating above the Oba. They are Portuguese traders, and the plaques themselves are made from the raw brass that the Portuguese traded with the Ebo in exchange for pepper, ivory, and gold. During the sixteenth, seventeenth, and eighteenth centuries, the Portuguese were also heavily involved in the Atlantic slave trade, as were the British and French. The west African coast was sometimes called the slave coast.

AFRICA

11

12

12: Ivory mask

Sixteenth century CE

This mask pendant is said to represent Idia, the queen mother of Oba Esigie, who lived around 1504–1550 CE. The Oba of Benin performs a variety of rituals to bring good fortune to his people, and Oba Esigie most likely wore this mask during rituals to honor his mother. It would have been placed either around his neck or on his hip. The small heads at the top represent Portuguese traders.

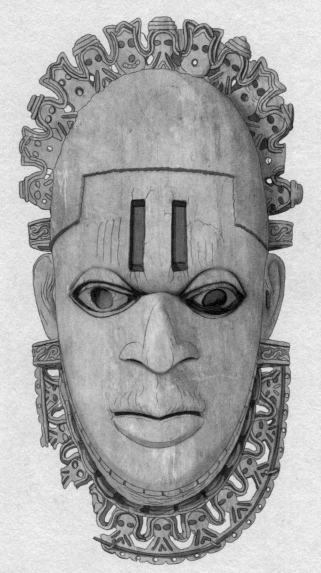

Ancient Egypt

The civilization of ancient Egypt began in oases on the banks of the river Nile in the northeast African desert. The Nile provided Egypt's all-important floodplain for growing crops and also functioned as a major travel and trade route.

People began to farm the Nile Valley from as early as the sixth millennium BCE. In the fourth millennium BCE, early farming villages developed into Egypt's first towns. Egypt was united under one ruler in around 3000 BCE, then ruled by pharaohs for the next three thousand years. There were three main periods of the pharaohs' rule, referred to as the Old Kingdom (2628–2181 BCE), the Middle Kingdom (2055–1650 BCE), and the New Kingdom (1550–1069 BCE).

The tremendous achievements of the ancient Egyptians are preserved in their art and monuments, in particular their pyramids, temples, and rock tombs. The afterlife was a preoccupation of the Egyptians, and the wealthy elite followed elaborate funerary rites in the hope of being granted eternal life.

The Egyptian people believed that only the gods could keep order in this world and that the pharaoh was a living representation of the gods. He ran the country through an organized system of government. Everyone paid taxes, either in goods or by working for the government, often on one of the pharaoh's major building projects.

During the New Kingdom, Egypt became the wealthiest, most powerful country in the ancient world. Although its strength then waned, its culture continued, even under foreign invaders, including the Greeks and Romans. When the Roman Empire officially became Christian in the fourth century CE, it ordered the Egyptian temples closed, marking an end to ancient Egypt.

Key to plate

13: Gilded outer coffin of Henutmehyt
Around 1250 BCE
Henutmehyt was a priestess from the Egyptian city of Thebes, and it is clear from her lavish burial that she was extremely wealthy and highly regarded. Tombs and coffins were only ever for the rich; the poor were simply buried in the sand. Henutmehyt's body was mummified, a lengthy process for preservation that involved internal organs being removed and the body dried out and wrapped in special bandages. Her mummy was then placed in a gold-leafed inner coffin inside this decorative outer coffin. Both coffins depict idealized versions of the priestess, designed to provide her spirit with a substitute body should her mummified body perish.

14: Miniature broad collar
332–222 BCE
The Egyptians took great pride in their appearance, wearing fine linen, elaborate hairstyles and colorful, striking jewelry. This miniature collar, made of gold and semiprecious stones, is likely to have been made as an offering to the gods. Religious offerings were a daily ritual in ancient Egypt. Ordinary people would make small offerings to shrines in their own homes, and priests would make three food offerings a day to the statues in their temples. The pharaoh, as supreme priest of all temples, would make the most important offerings of all.

15: Inlay depicting "Horus of Gold"
Fourth century BCE
This inlay is one of a group found at the site of the ancient city of Hermopolis. It is thought they formed a large inscription, listing the names of a king. Written words were deemed extremely powerful by the Egyptians, and they were beautifully sculpted on monuments in picture writing known as hieroglyphs. The Egyptians called this writing "the words of the gods." Egyptian kings chose their names very carefully, and these names were steeped in meaning. This hieroglyph depicts the name "Horus of Gold." The falcon god Horus was closely associated with the Egyptian pharaohs.

16: Ram's head amulet
712–664 BCE
This amulet comes from the period when Egypt was ruled by the Kushite kings. The kingdom of Kush was in Nubia, to the south of Egypt. During the 25th Dynasty, the Kushites ruled Egypt for around a hundred years. Images of Kushite pharaohs show them wearing rams' head amulets similar to this one. The ancient Egyptians associated the ram with fertility and with the god Amun, who had been adopted as the king of gods during the Middle Kingdom. Amulets were worn to bring good fortune and to ward off evil.

17

AFRICA

Key to plate

17: Painted wooden canopic jars
Around 700 BCE
During mummification, the intestines, stomach, lungs, and liver were removed, preserved, then stored in special containers called canopic jars. It was traditional for the stoppers of the jars to represent the four sons of the god Horus, with the heads of a baboon, a jackal, a falcon, and a human. Later, the preserved organs were stored inside the body, but the canopic jars continued to be included as important elements for a proper burial.

18: Wooden model of bakers at work
Around 1900 BCE
Bread was an important part of every Egyptian's diet. Farmers grew wheat on the fertile land along the Nile River. It was ground into flour, then mixed with water and baked, both on a small scale at home and on a more industrial scale to feed workers.

Models like this one were placed in tombs to represent the activities essential to everyday life — activities that were expected to be necessary in the next life as well.

19: Painted wooden model of a harp
1550–1069 BCE
This tomb model is another example of an object taken to the grave for use in the next life. Wall paintings show men and women making music and dancing as part of Egyptian banquet scenes.

20: Bust of Queen Nefertiti
Around 1340 BCE
Nefertiti was the wife of Akhenaten, the pharaoh who replaced the worship of Amun with worship of Aten, the god of the sun. Nefertiti was a prominent queen, ruling alongside her husband and playing an active role in his religious reforms. Her name translates as "a beautiful woman has

come," and her beauty is evident in this bust. It was found in the ruins of a sculptor's workshop in Amarna, the capital city founded by Akhenaten. This bust would have served as a model for artists to copy.

21: Page from the *Book of the Dead* of Hunefer
Around 1300 BCE
This scene is from a *Book of the Dead* produced for the royal scribe Hunefer. These books contained depictions of burial and funeral rites designed to achieve a safe passage to the next life. They were made for people of high rank and placed in their tombs. This scene shows priests performing rituals over Hunefer's mummified body while his wife and daughter mourn. The book is made of papyrus, the world's first paper-like material, which was made from strips of papyrus reed.

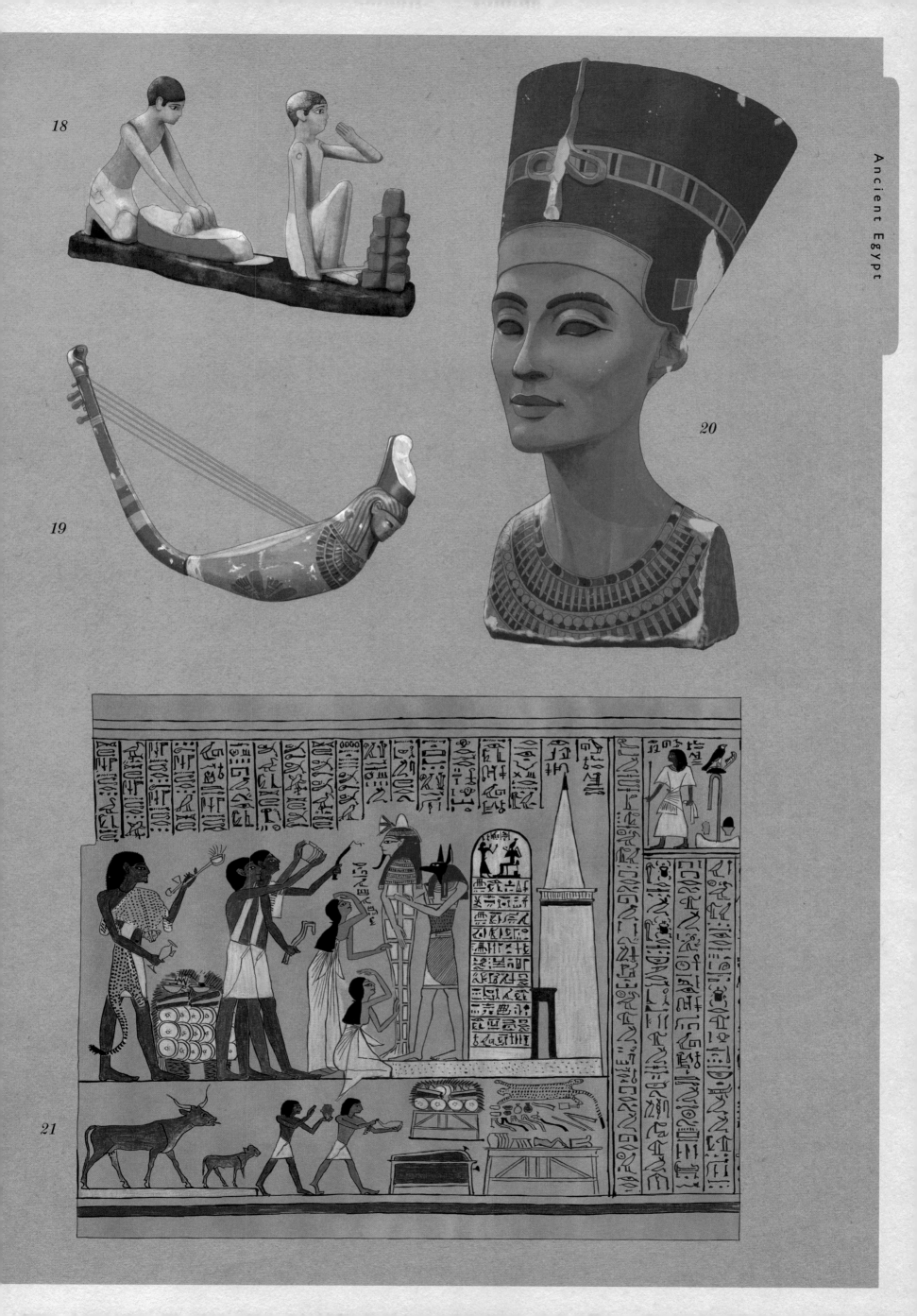

18

19

20

21

22: Fragment of a wall relief from tomb of Djehutyhotep
Around 1850 BCE
This figure is the first in a row of women that may have been the sisters of the deceased, a governor named Djehutyhotep. As is customary in Egyptian relief art, the woman's shoulders are facing forward while her legs and head are turned to the side.

23: Gold amulet of a lion
Around 1650–1550 BCE
Amulets were small, precious objects that were thought to bring power and protection. Animals were a common amulet design, and the lion was a symbol of power and kingship. The mane and face of

this lion show impressive detailing, especially considering that it is only 1½ inches/3.6 centimeters long. Egyptian metalwork dates back to at least the third millennium BCE.

24: Faïence vase in the form of Eros riding a duck
Around 300–250 BCE
This exquisite vase features Eros, the Greek god of love. It is made of an ancient type of glazed ceramic called faïence and was probably made in Alexandria, the city founded as Egypt's capital by Alexander the Great in 332 BCE. After Alexander's death, Egypt was ruled by the Ptolemies, a Greek dynasty, for nearly three hundred years. Alexandria was

home to one of the largest libraries in the ancient world and, as a port city, played an important role in transmitting Greek culture.

25: Gilded mummy mask
Late first century BCE to early first century CE
Mummy masks were placed inside Egyptian coffins over the face and shoulders of the mummy. The Egyptians believed that the spirit of the deceased could leave the tomb and that upon its return it would use the mummy mask to identify the correct body. Mummy masks were rarely made as accurate portraits. They followed the idealized style typical of Egyptian art, including

AFRICA

standard proportions for the depictions of human figures. The gilding on this mask relates to the sun god Re, whose flesh was said to be of pure gold. It was hoped that the deceased would be united with Re in the afterlife.

26: Heart scarab of Hatnefer
Around 1492–1473 BCE

The Egyptians believed that their hearts were weighed after death by the god Anubis and that only those with a light, virtuous heart were granted passage to the next life. Amulets in the form of scarab beetles, called heart scarabs, often accompanied the deceased to their tombs as good-luck charms. The scarab, or dung beetle, was a powerful symbol of rebirth and therefore a prominent feature of funerary art. Just as the young scarabs took flight from the dung ball, so the sun god rose up into the heavens, and so the Egyptians hoped they themselves would live on in death. This exquisite heart scarab is inscribed with a passage from a *Book of the Dead*: a plea from the deceased, Hatnefer, to her own heart not to let her down.

27: Faïence *wedjat* eye
1069–945 BCE

The *wedjat* eye, also known as the Eye of Horus, was an Egyptian healing symbol and a very popular amulet design. It originates from the story of the god Horus, who lost his left eye in battle and had it restored by the goddess Hathor. Blue and green were common colors for *wedjat* amulets as they symbolized regeneration.

28: Statue of two men and a boy
1353–1336 BCE

This small statue shows a man of high status next to a younger man and a boy. The statue was most likely a domestic icon, used for veneration in the home. The family was at the heart of Egyptian society, and it is possible that these three figures represent a grandfather, father, and son.

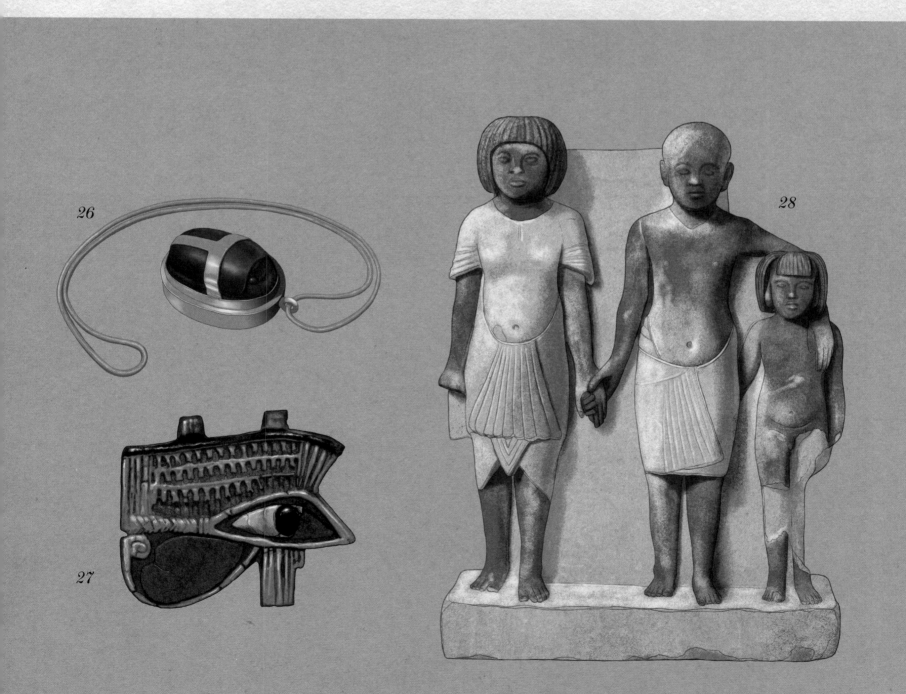

26

27

28

Gallery 2

America

The Olmec

The Olmec civilization thrived in southern Mexico from around 1200 to 400 BCE. Its people cultivated the land along coastal lowlands and were mainly corn farmers who benefited from the annual river floods that irrigated and fertilized their soil. Abundant harvests enabled major centers to develop—notably San Lorenzo and La Venta—and these sites became home to Mesoamerica's first complex societies.

Although much about the Olmec remains a mystery, their civilization is seen by many as the mother culture of Mesoamerica. Archaeological finds include stepped platforms leading to temples, ritual offerings, intricate sculptures, and the first evidence of a sport known only as the Ball Game that became popular across Mesoamerica. What the Olmec called themselves is unknown. The Aztecs later named them Olmec, which in the Nahuatl language means "people who live in the rubber-producing region." The Olmec extracted latex from rubber trees to make objects such as balls.

Archaeological evidence suggests that the Olmec were spiritual people who saw the power of the gods through forces of nature such as freshwater springs. Intriguing Olmec cave paintings of supernatural beings remain to this day, as do sculptures of all sizes, from small statuettes to massive altars and heads. Many were crafted to venerate the gods, to signify power, or to provide protection. The Olmec also used earth or, more rarely, stone to build huge religious centers in their settlements, and the first Mesoamerican pyramid was built at La Venta. Although the Olmec ceased to be a dominant culture around 400 BCE, their strong imagery and customs profoundly influenced both the Maya and the Aztecs.

Key to plate

1: **Seated female figurine**
900–500 BCE
The human form was the most common subject for Olmec sculpture, but very few stone sculptures of women have been found. This small jade figurine, dressed in a skirt, stands at only 3 inches/7.7 centimeters tall and is remarkably detailed given how hard jade is to carve. Jade was prized by the Olmec for its color, shine, and durability. It was also very scarce and had to be imported from around 370 miles/600 kilometers away. Precious jade objects have been discovered in Olmec burial sites.

The green jade of this figurine has been stained with the reddish mineral ore cinnabar, probably to help the carving stand out. It was discovered in a burial chamber in La Venta, along with other precious items, including a mirror made of polished hematite (a reddish-black mineral). This figure also features a tiny hematite mirror on its chest. Mirrors were seen as powerful symbolic objects by the Olmec as well as by the Maya and Aztecs after them.

2: **Colossal head, number five**
1200–900 BCE
This is one of seventeen colossal stone heads found in Mexico, ten of them at the site of San Lorenzo. They are numbered by the order in which they were found, and they range in height from 5 feet/1.5 meters to 11 feet/ 3.4 meters. The heads follow a similar design: relatively flat faces with large features shallowly carved, yet the distinctive facial features of each one indicate that they are unique portraits of real people, most probably Olmec rulers. They all wear striking headgear, and one theory is that these are protective helmets, perhaps worn for war or to take part in a ceremonial ball game.

The stone for these heads came from the mountains and had to be transported over long distances—up to 50 miles/80 kilometers. It may well have been carried along rivers, strapped to large wooden rafts. One suggestion is that the stone was originally used as a massive altar for a ruler, then later sculpted into the ruler's head, perhaps to mark a rite of passage or to commemorate his death. The sheer scale of the heads suggests that they were a display of power, and the immense effort required to create them is evidence of a dominant ruler with a workforce at his command.

1

2

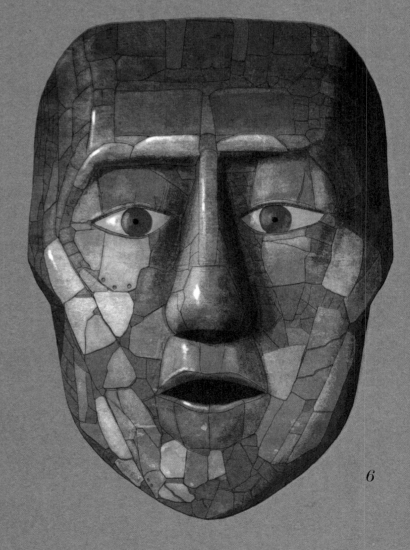

3

4

5

6

AMERICA

The Maya

The Mayan civilization rose to prominence around 250 CE. Its people never formed a single empire but lived in city-state kingdoms dotted across present-day southern Mexico, Guatemala, northern Belize, western Honduras, and El Salvador. What brought the Maya together as a culture was a shared belief system, similar societal structures, and similar styles of art and architecture.

The Maya settled in villages as early as 650 BCE. Their cities began as ceremonial centers. Successive rulers added to the cities, building stone temples, palaces, pyramids, ball-game courts, and plazas. The lifestyles of the royal family, aristocrats, priests, and craftsmen in the city were sustained by the corn, squash, and beans grown in the surrounding terraced fields.

Central to Mayan life was a desire to please and appease the gods through rituals and ceremonies. People believed that the gods required regular offerings, in particular human blood and sacrifices, to maintain order on earth. Priests studied the heavens for a deeper understanding of the supernatural and became excellent astronomers and mathematicians.

Hieroglyphic writing carved on the stone buildings has revealed much of what we know about the Maya. Their cities are now overgrown ruins, but around six million Maya descendants still live in the same region, mostly in small village communities, and some seventy Mayan languages are spoken.

Key to plate

3: Vessel with a procession of warriors
750–850 CE
The naked figure on this vessel is a prisoner being led to a ritual sacrifice. At the head of the procession is a Mayan ruler, identifiable by his jaguar pelt, a symbol of power and authority. He carries a bloodied weapon and has an instrument for bloodletting in his headdress. Even the Mayan rulers would submit themselves to bloodletting when making special requests to the gods. The painting on this vessel is one of the few surviving examples of the colorful scenes that would have covered the walls of ancient Mayan cities.

4: Incense burner
Fourth century CE
This ceramic incense burner shows a Mayan king sitting cross-legged and wearing an elaborate headdress. The headdress formed part of the king's ceremonial dress, identifying him as

the gods' representative on earth and suggesting his own divine status. It was thought that the living king could communicate with the gods and that he would join them when he died. Smoke from burning incense was also thought to reach the gods and carry offerings to them.

5: Pair of ear flare frontals
Third to sixth century CE
These jade ear ornaments measure 2 inches/5 centimeters across and would have been attached to a short shaft and worn in a wide hole in the earlobe. They are carved with a motif based on petals or leaves. Many figures in Mayan art are shown wearing this type of ear ornament, including the incense-burner king in this gallery. Jade was a symbol of wealth, since it was rare and very difficult to carve.

6: Jade mosaic funerary mask
683 CE
This mask, which belonged to Pakal

the Great, called Janaahb' Pakal (Radiant Shield Sun), was discovered in a royal tomb beneath the Temple of Inscriptions at the ancient city of Palenque. The inscriptions of the tomb provide a written history of Pakal's dynasty and rule. According to them, he became king at the age of twelve and ruled until his death, in 683 CE, at the age of eighty. Studies of his bones, however, suggest he was actually forty-five or fifty when he died.

Under Pakal's reign, Palenque was transformed into a major Mayan city; he commissioned the Temple of Inscriptions, built on a massive pyramid structure, as his own burial place. Pyramids were intended to replicate the surrounding mountains, where deities and ancestors were thought to reside. Jade was highly prized by the Maya, in particular jade of a bright-green color. This mask gave Pakal a youthful face, suggestive of the Mayan corn god, for the afterlife.

The Aztecs

The Aztecs, or Mexica, lived in the Valley of Mexico from the twelfth century CE. According to Aztec belief, the Aztec people originated as a small, wandering tribe and were guided to the valley by their main god, Huitzilopochtli, who led them to settle on an island in the marshes of Lake Texcoco. Here they founded their capital, the city of Tenochtitlán, around 1325 CE. A swampy landscape seems an unlikely setting for the development of Mesoamerica's last great native empire, but the Aztecs learned to grow food on artificial floating islands and gradually expanded their realm through waging war and forging alliances. Tenochtitlán became one of the largest cities in the world and was supported by an efficient system of trade and tribute.

Central to Aztec life was a sense of duty to the gods who had set the world in motion. Like the Olmec, the Maya, and the Toltecs (a tribe who dominated central Mexico in the tenth to twelfth centuries CE) before them, the Aztecs believed that blood offerings were necessary to appease the gods and sustain life on earth. Ceremonial wars were fought with the sole purpose of sacrificing any captives on top of steep temple pyramids. The Aztec word for blood literally means "treasured water." Priests would wrench the heart out of a prisoner and let his blood flow onto the soil below to encourage the rains to fall and the earth to be fertile.

The Aztecs were led by an elected emperor who was both the head of the army and chief priest. Revered by his people, he held divine status and was said to communicate directly with the gods. Each new emperor proved his might by waging war and winning new territories. By the early sixteenth century, the empire included 489 city-states and covered most of modern-day central and southern Mexico.

When Hernán Cortés arrived with a small Spanish army in 1519 CE, he was astounded by the Aztecs' wealth and infrastructure. However, the mighty Aztecs had no experience of Spanish military tactics and weaponry. Two years later, the Aztec capital lay in ruins and the Aztec lands became a Spanish colony.

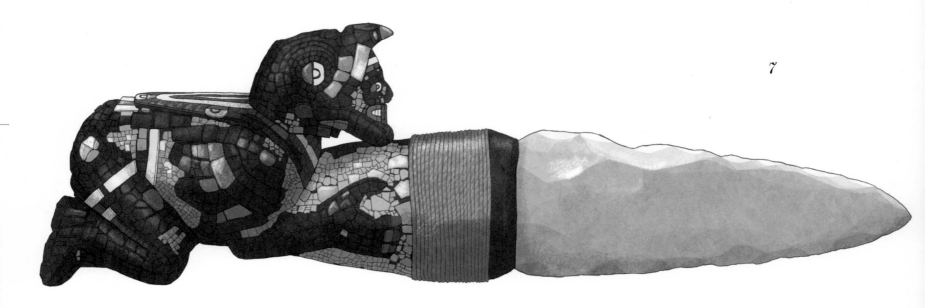

7

Key to plate

7: Mosaic ceremonial knife

Fifteenth–sixteenth century CE

The wooden handle of this knife is carved in the shape of a warrior and decorated with tiny pieces of turquoise, shell, and malachite (a green mineral). The warrior figure wears an eagle headdress, the sign of an elite group of Aztec warriors, and appears to be holding the flint blade of the knife in place. Warriors would have fought with much plainer knives than this one; the more ornate designs were reserved for making ritual sacrifices or use in ceremonies. There were two orders of high-ranking Aztec warriors, the Eagle and the Jaguar. Young men had to perform at least twenty deeds of bravery before they could join the ranks of these orders.

8: Sun stone

1250–1521 CE

This intricately carved sun stone was once part of a temple complex in Tenochtitlán. It is also known as the calendar stone, because it features the twenty Aztec day names that formed the basis of their sacred calendar.

The Aztecs had two calendars, following a tradition that probably dated back to the Olmec. Like the Mayan calendar, the Aztec sacred calendar was 260 days long and mostly used for divination. The Aztecs also had a 365-day solar calendar, primarily to mark civic events such as religious festivals and the farming seasons.

At the center of the sun stone is the face of an Aztec sun god, surrounded by representations of the four previous world ages. The Aztecs believed they lived in the fifth and last of the world ages, which began when the city of Tenochtitlán was founded. According to Aztec mythology, each age was made and destroyed by the gods and had a different god serving as its sun.

9: Pot depicting Tláloc

Fifteenth century CE

Tláloc was the Aztecs' rain god and one of their most important deities. He decided whether to send rain or hail, cause floods or drought, make a good harvest or ruin the crops. The Aztecs believed Tláloc stored water in four massive jars, one at each point of the compass. On this pot the figure of Tláloc is painted blue to symbolize water and is wearing a pointed headdress to represent the mountains, a precious source of water.

8

9

10

Key to plate

10: **Double-headed serpent mosaic**
Fifteenth or sixteenth century CE
The serpent held deep significance for the Aztec people. Many of their gods took the form of a serpent, including the feathered serpent Quetzalcóatl, patron of priests and symbol of death

and resurrection. Serpents were also a living example of regeneration every time they shed their skins.

Around two thousand tiny pieces of turquoise have been meticulously arranged on carved wood to form this serpent. Turquoise was favored

over jade by the Aztecs, though both were prized for their color. Turquoise evoked new growth, water, and the feathers of the quetzal, which were worn in ceremonies by priests. Both the color green and serpents signified fertility, and ensuring the land would

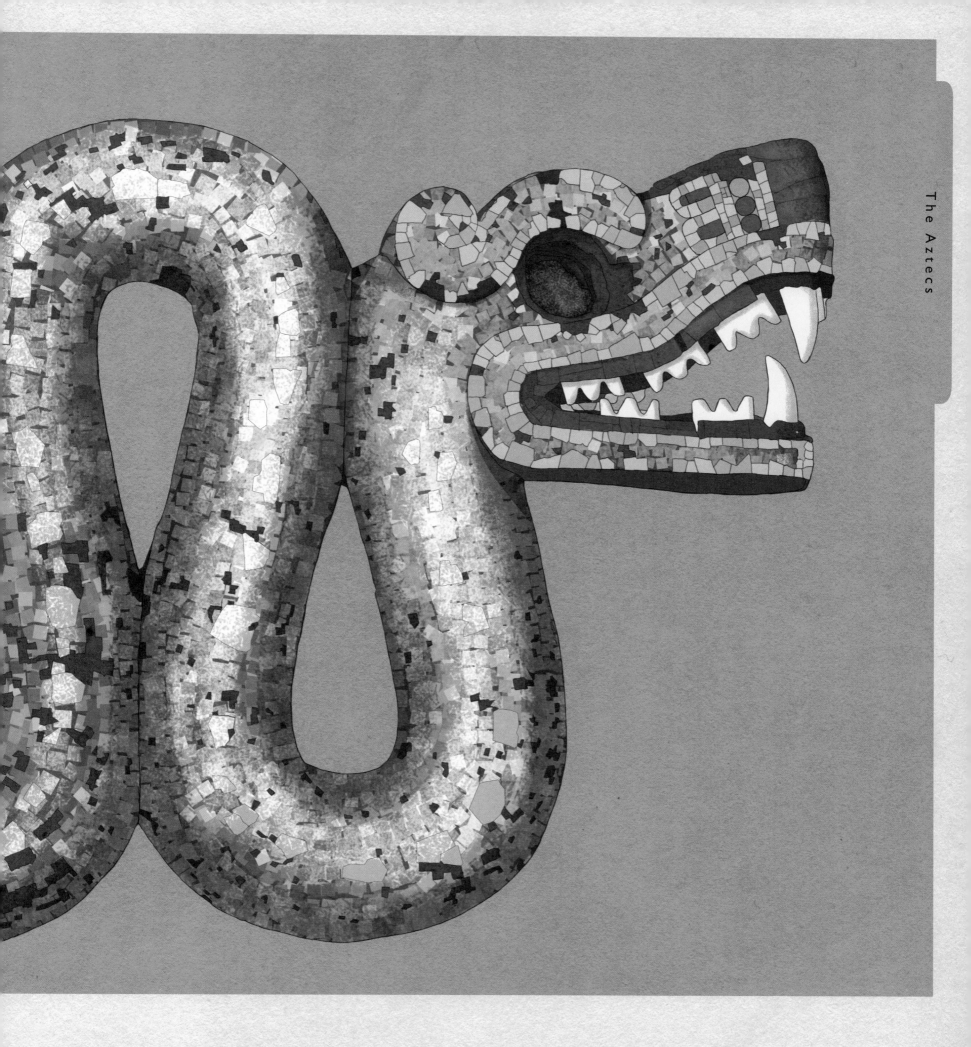

remain fertile was at the heart of most religious ceremonies. It is highly likely that this serpent was worn during human sacrifices, on the chest of an important priest or even the emperor. The bright turquoise skin and open jaws—picked out in red and white

shell—were intended to both impress and terrify the beholder.

The craftsmen best known for their turquoise mosaics were not Aztecs but Mixtecs. At the height of the Aztec Empire, many Mixtec towns came under Aztec rule and had to pay

tribute to the emperor, including gifts of gold and turquoise. This serpent would have made a valuable item of tribute—an example of the fearsome power the Aztecs held and the high demands they could make.

The Hopewell

The Hopewell culture prospered in and around what is now the midwestern United States from 100 BCE to 500 CE, a period known as the Middle Woodland. The term Hopewell is used to describe a wide scattering of people who lived near rivers in temporary settlements of one to three households and practiced a mixture of hunting, gathering, and crop growing. Hopewell settlements were linked by extensive and complex trading routes, which doubled as communication networks, bringing people together for important ceremonies.

The predominant surviving features of the Hopewell culture are its large burial mounds and earthworks (large, raised earth structures). Hopewell mounds were enormous: the largest site at the Newark Earthworks in Ohio, called the Octagon, covers more than fifty acres. Hopewell earthworks are also notable for their precise, interconnected geometric shapes and the mathematical precision with which they were measured and positioned in relation to one another. The straight and parallel lines of the earthworks suggest a direct relationship with the positions of the moon, stars, and sun, and the Octagon is now known to act as an observatory for watching the 18.6-year lunar cycle.

Precious burial goods have been found in some of the mounds. These include objects of adornment made from copper, mica, and obsidian, imported to the region from hundreds of miles away. Stone and ceramics were also fashioned into intricate shapes.

After 400 CE, the Hopewell culture began to decline. The invention of the bow and arrow may have led people to live in larger, more permanent communities for protection as warfare became more deadly. With fewer people using the trade routes, there was no longer a network linking people to the Hopewell traditions.

Key to plate

11: Dog pipe
100–200 CE

Hundreds of pipes sculpted from stone into intricate representations of animals—from owls and herons to beavers and toads—have been found buried in Hopewell mounds. The natural pose of the dog in this beautifully crafted object shows that whoever made it was a keen observer of nature. Pipes provided an important link to the spiritual world. Shamans would smoke their pipes to induce a trance-like state for their healing rituals. The sculpted pipe animals would face the shaman as he smoked and take on the role of his spirit guide or a messenger from the deities. The ritual of sharing a pipe with a new acquaintance was also used along trade routes to signify peaceful intentions.

12: The Wray Figurine
100 BCE–400 CE

This small stone sculpture was found on the ancient cemetery of the Newark Earthworks during construction on the site in the nineteenth century CE. It is thought to be of a shaman—a spiritual leader and healer. The shaman is wearing a bearskin and appears to be in the middle of a transformation, either into a bear spirit or back to his human state. In his lap he holds a human head, perhaps in readiness for burial or to use in an act of divination. The Hopewell respected bears for their ferocity and for walking on two legs like a human. Their ability to wake from a long hibernation made them a powerful symbol of rebirth and a fitting subject for a burial object.

13: Mica hand
100 BCE–400 CE

The shiny mineral mica was used to make Hopewell ceremonial objects. It occurs in layers that can be carefully prised into thin, fragile, almost transparent sheets. Artisans cut the sheets into geometric and animal shapes as well as human outlines. Thicker pieces were used as mirrors by spiritual leaders, and some much larger slabs have been found in burial mounds. Mica was transported from the Appalachian Mountains, over 300 miles/480 kilometers away, perhaps in a trade exchange with other Middle Woodland people or as offerings from pilgrims coming to see the great earthworks. This delicately shaped hand is almost twice the size of a real hand, measuring over 11 inches/28 centimeters high and 6 inches/15 centimeters wide. Two piercings suggest that it was attached to another object for display, perhaps to be carried or worn as part of a ceremony.

14: Projectile points
200 BCE–500 CE

Fashioned out of flint and chert, varieties of stone that form sharp edges when broken, these points would have been used as knives or scrapers. The largest is 2 inches/5.1 centimeters long. Their distinctive shapes have enabled archaeologists to identify various Hopewell settlements and to estimate the population of each one.

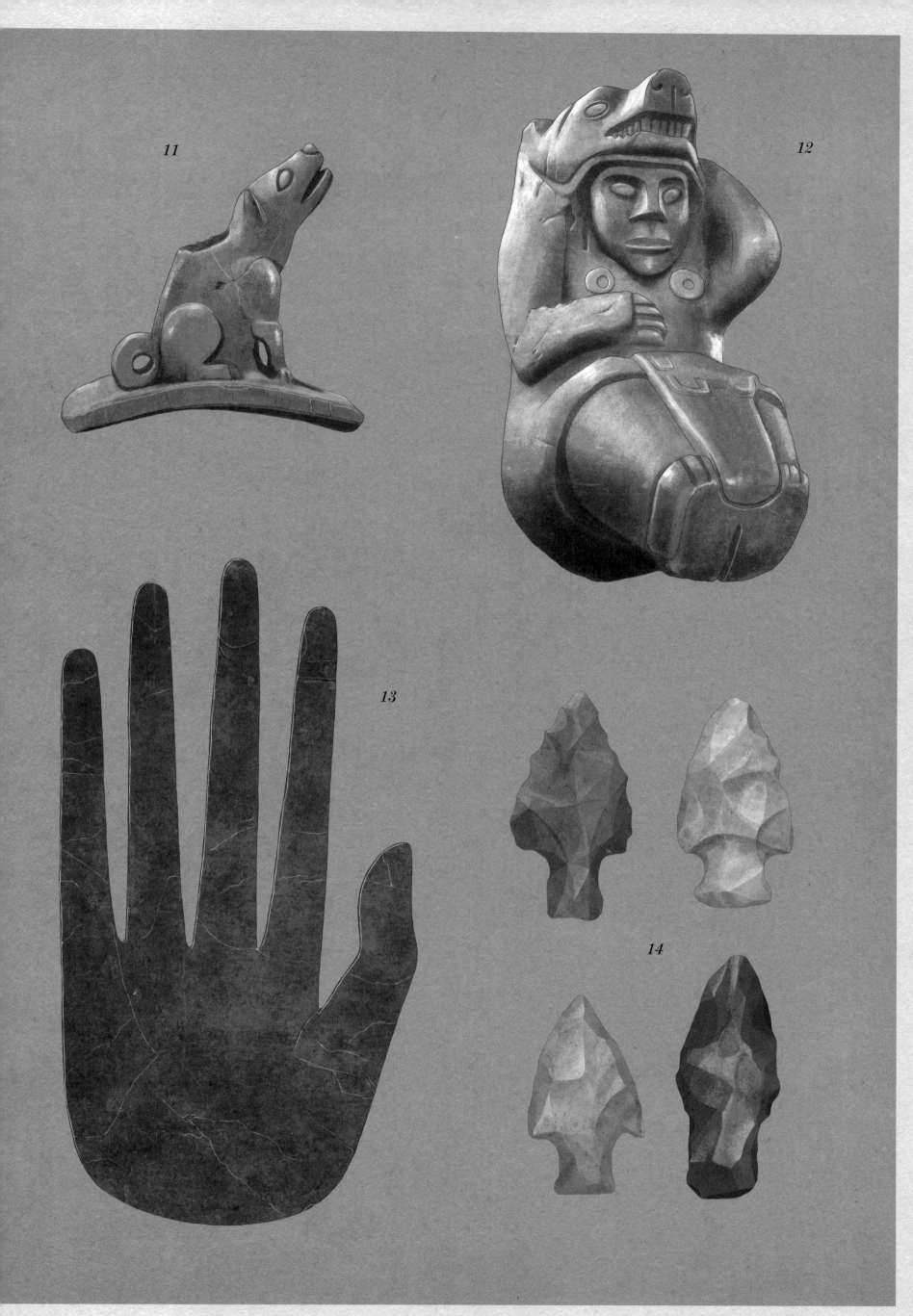

The Pueblo

Pueblo ancestry is shared by more than 75,000 Native Americans living in the southwestern United States today. The Ancestral Pueblo lived on the Colorado plateau and made use of the area's rocky mesas, cliff faces, and canyons to construct settlements.

The name Pueblo, meaning "villagers," was adopted by Spanish explorers in the sixteenth century to distinguish these settled, agricultural communities from neighboring nomadic peoples. There was never a single Pueblo people, and, while many Pueblo communities have shared beliefs and customs, there are six very different Pueblo languages being spoken today. The nomadic tribes had their own name for the Pueblo that is also still used today: Anasazi, which means "enemy people" in the Navajo language.

The Pueblo did not always live in settlements. During early stages of their history, known as the Basketmaker Periods (100–750 CE), the Pueblo relied more on hunting and gathering than agriculture and wove baskets to carry their possessions and supplies. As they increased their farming activities and became more settled, transportation was less important and baskets were gradually replaced with pottery.

Early Pueblo dwellings were caves or shallow pit houses. Later (800–1300 CE), living units and storage rooms were built in stone and then added to—rather like apartment complexes today. Some buildings, known as Great Houses, ended up four stories high, with as many as eight hundred rooms. Earlier pit houses were often incorporated into the Great Houses and enlarged into community or ceremonial rooms called kivas.

The Pueblo traded with other cultures and communities for goods, including shell beads from the Pacific coast, copper bells from western Mexico, and turquoise from other Pueblo mines. A severe drought in the late thirteenth century and increased conflict with nomadic tribes led the Pueblo people to move south and east in search of more fertile lands. Seventeenth-century Spanish colonizers brought contagious diseases and more conflict, which further depleted communities. Despite that, modern Pueblo cultures, languages, and traditional arts and crafts are strong, and there are more than thirty thriving Pueblo communities that number more than 60,000 individuals.

Key to plate

15: Cylinder jar
900–1130 CE
Ancestral Pueblo pottery was made using the same coil-and-scrape technique that is practiced by the Pueblo today. Potters begin with a flattened base and build up from it in clay coils, scraping and shaping along the way. The coils are smoothed and coated with watery clay slip before being decorated and fired on a carefully controlled bonfire. This cylinder jar was found at the impressive D-shaped Great Building at Pueblo Bonito, in New Mexico.

16: Mortar with textile designs
900–1100 CE
This stone mortar was also found at Pueblo Bonito. It would have been used with a pestle for grinding pigments to make paint. The mortar itself is painted with a stepped geometric design characteristic of Pueblo weavings and textiles. It probably originated from early Pueblo basket designs, which were influenced by the fact that straight lines and right angles are easier to weave than curves. It is unknown whether the patterns had specific meanings, although some may have signified a particular clan.

17: Jug
Twelfth to eighteenth century CE
Traditionally, Pueblo potters were women. Some Pueblo communities were matriarchal, meaning property, farmland, and clan affiliation were inherited through the mother. Likewise, pottery skills and designs were passed from mother to daughter. Each Pueblo settlement would try to keep the location of its clay deposit a secret, to prevent it from being plundered. Items such as this jug, with its striking geometric patterns, were intended for everyday use rather than display. Only from the late nineteenth century was pottery made specifically for tourists and collectors. Most Pueblo potters today are women, and they often refer to the clay as female, with names such as Grandmother Clay or Mother Earth.

15

16   *17*

HISTORIUM

Gallery 3

Asia

Ancient India
Ancient China
Ancient Japan
Ancient Korea

Ancient India

The Indian subcontinent was home to some of the oldest and most influential civilizations in the world.

India gets its name from the Indus River, which runs through modern-day Pakistan. It was along this river that the first great ancient Indian civilization, the Indus Valley civilization, emerged between 3300 and 1300 BCE. Protected by mountains to the north, jungles to the east, and ocean to the south and west, and containing the cities of Mohenjo-Daro and Harappa, the Indus Valley provided an ideal place for human society to thrive.

In the second millennium BCE, the Indus Valley civilization went into decline. It was followed by the Vedic Period, named after the Vedas, religious texts composed during that time. The Vedas were written in archaic Sanskrit and include hymns recited during rituals that praised a wide range of gods.

Modern Hinduism finds some of its oldest roots in the Vedic religion, continuing some of the Vedic rituals and sharing many of its deities. By contrast, Buddhism and Jainism developed as a reaction against the strict Vedic hierarchy and its elaborate sacrifices. Buddhism was established in the fifth century BCE by the teacher Siddhartha Gautama, known as the Buddha, meaning "enlightened one." Jainism was founded by a contemporary of the Buddha known as Mahavira, meaning "great hero." In the first century CE, Christianity was introduced to India, and in the eighth century CE, Islam arrived via Arab traders.

The diverse beliefs of ancient India are strongly represented in its arts, notably dancing, sculpture, painting, epic poetry, and architecture. In 1193 CE, Afghan armies successfully invaded India, leading to a period of Islamic occupation and a new period of cultural history.

Key to plate

1: **Statue of Ganesha**

Eleventh century CE

The elephant-headed god, Ganesha, is one of many Hindu deities. He is the son of the god Shiva and his consort Parvati. At the heart of Hinduism is the belief in a single, divine unity, a supreme truth called *brahman.* All gods and goddesses are aspects of *brahman,* some with shifting identities and numerous incarnations. It is believed that a wise man named Vyasa dictated epic poems to Ganesha over a period of two and a half years. The result was an important Hindu text, the epic poems of the *Mahabharata.*

The oldest known statues of divinities in India are Vedic and Buddhist. They date from the second and first centuries BCE and include the first carved images of Buddha. These early statues owe much to Greek art. Alexander the Great invaded India around 327 BCE, establishing several Greek settlements, and an Indo-Greek kingdom was later founded in the north of the subcontinent.

By the fourth century CE, Buddhist and Hindu art were developing side by side, in strikingly similar, stylized ways. Ever since, Hindu, Jain, and Buddhist statues or images have needed to conform to an archetype in order to be suitable for worship. Strict instructions dictate how to execute the artworks, and it is very unusual for an individual artist's style to emerge.

Hindu statues are seen as a vessel for the divine. They form part of the belief that the physical universe is an illusion, masking a divine reality. During a ceremony, priests invoke the spirit of the deity to enter the statue, allowing worshippers a glimpse of the divine.

1

2: Indus dancing girl
Around 2500 BCE

Standing only 4 inches/10.5 centimeters high, this statue is a remarkable artifact from Mohenjo-Daro, one of the two great cities of the Indus Valley civilization. It shows that craftsmen of the time not only knew how to make and cast bronze, but also had the artistic ability to capture a figure in a natural, informal pose. The choice of a dancer as a statue is evidence of a cultural interest in the performing arts, while her bracelets and necklace suggest a desire for adornment.

The Indus Valley civilization left no written histories, but archaeological evidence describes an organized society, with communal granaries, a grid pattern of city planning, flood defenses, artisans working in metals, ivory, and wood, and trading links with Mesopotamia and Egypt. The Indus Valley culture flourished for over six hundred years, and its disappearance may have been caused by invasion or by a rise in sea level that damaged the civilization's trade. Or it may have been a combination of the two.

3: Carved steatite seals
2600–1900 BCE

These small, square seals have been carved in soft soapstone and baked so they harden and whiten. They are the first evidence of writing in ancient India, although the meanings of the pictographic symbols have yet to be determined. Thousands of seals have been found in Mohenjo-Daro and Harappa, as well as in places on the Indus trade routes. The Indus Valley culture is the first culture known to make cotton cloth, and evidence suggests that goods ready for trade were wrapped in the cotton, then closed with these seals. It is theorized that the symbols were a way of marking the goods.

4: Mother Goddess figurine
Third century BCE

This wide-hipped terra-cotta female figure belongs to a long tradition of worshipping the Mother Goddess. It may have been an icon in celebrations of fertility. Baked clay was widely used for artistic expression at the height of the Indus Valley civilization, 2600–2000 BCE, and during the time of the Mauryan Empire, 325–185 BCE. The importance of the Mother Goddess continued in later centuries when the wives and

ASIA

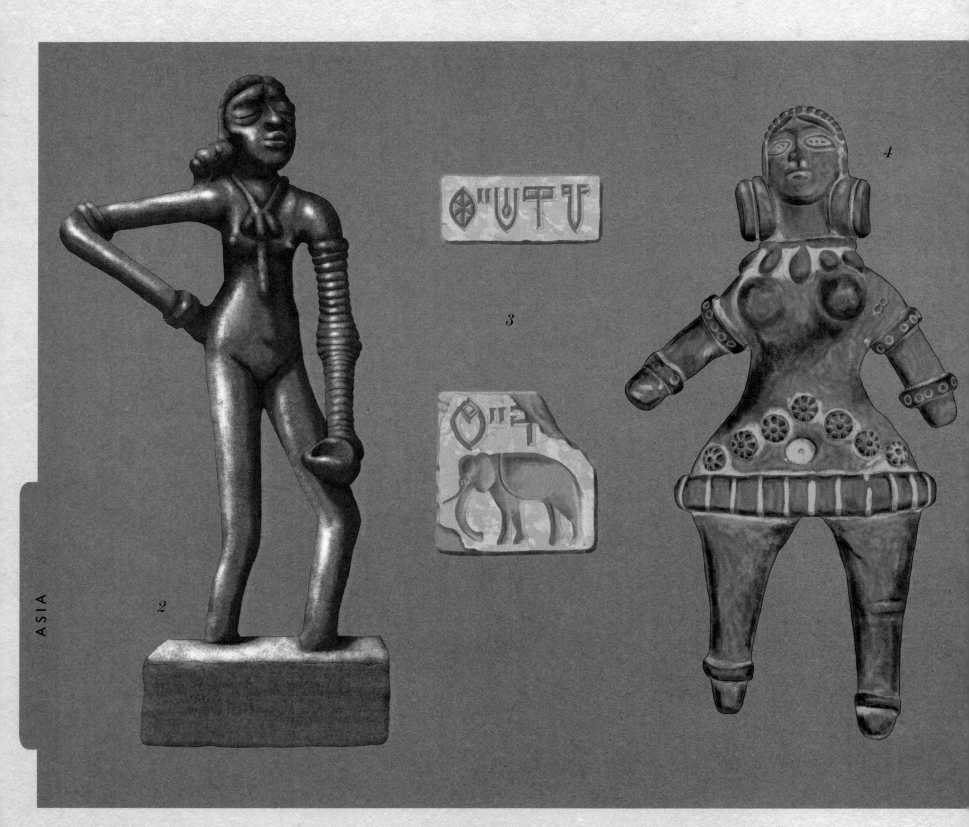

consorts of the major gods were all seen as aspects of the one great Mother Goddess. This figure provides evidence of sophisticated textile production in the culture, as the figure's dress is embroidered with floral patterns.

5: Ashoka's pillar
Around 238 BCE
This stone block is a fragment of one of the many pillars erected across the Mauryan Empire by Emperor Ashoka the Great. It is carved with a message announcing Ashoka's benevolent policy to all people and all faiths. Ashoka did not start his reign as a tolerant, peace-loving leader. He was a ruthless military man, seeking to expand his empire, until a particularly bloody assault led him to change his ways. Filled with remorse, Ashoka adopted Buddhism and the concept of *Dharma*—a sense of duty, piety, and selflessness. He wanted people across his empire to know about his change of heart and to feel safe once more. So, in an age when mass communication was almost impossible, Ashoka chose to erect stone pillars as a kind of public address system. They stood 30 feet/9 meters high and bore messages written in local dialects for all to understand.

6: Gold earrings
First century BCE
These beautifully crafted gold earrings are so heavy and large— 3 inches/7.6 centimeters wide— that they would have distended the earlobes and hung down to the shoulders. The quality of goldsmithing and the use of royal emblems (a winged lion and an elephant) make it highly likely that these earrings were royal commissions. Jewelry had been worn in ancient India for millennia. It was a sign of prestige and wealth.

Both male and female deities are depicted wearing earrings, bracelets, and necklaces.

7: Buddha head
Fifth century CE
This head would have been part of a seated Buddha statue. It was carved from sandstone during the Gupta Period, which lasted from 320 CE to the early sixth century CE, and shows the Buddha deep in meditation. Despite their earlier divide, Buddhism and Hinduism developed side by side during this time with some Hindus worshipping Buddha as an avatar of their god Vishnu and some Buddhists revering Hindu deities. The Gupta Period was a golden age in Indian history, when the arts and sciences flourished. Learning was encouraged by rulers, and a type of Buddhist monastery that functioned much like a university emerged.

5

6

7

Ancient China

China has the longest unbroken history of any great civilization. Its Neolithic Age can be traced back to 10,000 BCE, when farming settlements began to develop along the Yellow and Yangzi Rivers. China's famous pottery and jade carvings first emerged in these times.

From around 2100 BCE, China's history was shaped by the rise and fall of various dynasties. Little is known about the Xia Dynasty, but the subsequent Shang and Zhou Dynasties (1600–1046 BCE and 1045–256 BCE) combine to form China's Bronze Age. The existence of bronze ware and its ritual use offer evidence of an organized society.

Each dynasty varied in duration and territory, some gaining land, others losing it. The ruling families were continually threatened by internal rebellions and foreign invasions. Consecutive rulers would strive to prove their right to rule. By pointing to their illustrious ancestry and their success on the battlefield, they would claim to have the blessings of the heavens. To show their greatness, they surrounded themselves with magnificent objects, many of which accompanied them to the grave.

In the sixth and fifth centuries BCE, the great sage Confucius promoted a system of moral, social, and political thought that became known as Confucianism. The philosophy of Taoism was formed in the second and first centuries BCE, though its roots go back further. Buddhism was introduced from India in the first century BCE.

Most outside influences reached China along the Silk Road, a network of trade routes that linked China with central Asia and Africa. The road was named in honor of China's valued export, silk, the manufacture of which was a Chinese invention. Other significant Chinese inventions include gunpowder, the stirrup, paper, and printing.

8

8: Gold belt buckle

Second century BCE

This buckle is one of over two thousand objects recovered from a tomb at Shizishan, in western China. The tomb belonged to a Chu king who ruled during the Western Han Dynasty.

Tombs are by far the greatest source of ancient Chinese artifacts. Important men (and, more rarely, women) were buried with exquisite treasures to accompany them into the afterlife. The expertly executed image on this buckle is of a tiger and a bear attacking a horse.

The Western Han rulers were the first to forge an empire across the whole of China. Their dynasty was a golden age in which the arts and culture flourished. Models of houses and paintings found in the tombs give a sense of the impressive architecture of the time, as do the vaulted roofs of the tombs themselves.

9: Wine flask

Around third century BCE

This bronze flask, intricately decorated with silver inlay, is from the later years of the Eastern Zhou Dynasty, in what is known as the Warring States Period (475–221 BCE). Although, as the name suggests, it was a time of much fighting, it was also a period of technological and intellectual development. The craftsmanship involved in making this flask is astonishing. The meticulously designed geometrical patterns would have been indented during the casting process from the inside of its clay mold, then filled in with silver afterward. Bronzes were prized above silver and gold items, but this inlay technique gave the precious metals a place in Chinese metalworking of the period. Vessels such as this flask would have made lavish gifts, dowry offerings, or precious burial objects.

10: Gilt bronze Maitreya Buddha

486 CE

Buddhism reached China from India during the Han Dynasty, around the first century CE. Its rules for life and meditation techniques were familiar to many Chinese, as they resembled those of Taoism. As more of the Buddhist scriptures were translated for Chinese readers, the Buddhist faith became more developed and prominent. From the fourth to the sixth centuries CE, various dynasties adopted Buddhism as their state religion. This statue of the Maitreya Buddha, the teaching Buddha of the next cosmic era, is derived from Indian prototypes, but the dramatic folds in his drapery are particular to China in the late fifth century. The unusual patterning on the folds can be traced to Kucha, an important center on the Silk Road.

9

10

11

12

13

Key to plate

11: Earthenware bowl
3200–2700 BCE
Pottery has been made in China for more than 17,000 years. This bowl comes from the late Neolithic time, when the Yangshao culture flourished along the banks of the Yellow River. It was made by stacking coils of clay, then creating a smooth finish with paddles and scrapers. Flowing black lines against the exposed clay are typical of this period. Decorated vessels appear to have been reserved as burial objects rather than for everyday use.

12: Square cauldron
1300–1046 BCE
This ritual vessel is remarkable for its size and age. At 52 inches/ 133 centimeters high and weighing two thousand pounds/875 kilograms, it is one of the biggest bronze items ever excavated. Making a bronze vessel of these proportions would have taken an astonishing amount of time, effort, and manpower. It is all the more remarkable because it was discovered in the tomb of a woman: Fu Hao. To treat women with the same respect as men was extremely rare in ancient China, but Fu Hao was an extraordinary figure. In addition to being a wife of the Shang King, Wu Ding, she was a warrior, a politician, and the first known female military leader. Her tomb contains a rich treasure trove.

13: Dragon pendant
Fifth to fourth century BCE
The green gemstone jade was valued above all other materials in ancient China, and its status in Chinese culture continues to this day. Translucent and extremely hard, to the Chinese it symbolized purity and indestructibility. Expert craftsmen worked it into ornaments, ceremonial weapons, and ritual objects. Jade pendants were often strung with beads and worn by important men, hanging from the waist or shoulder. The dragon was also held in great esteem by the ancient Chinese. It was originally a rain deity and was thought to bring gifts from the heavens. The emperors later adopted the dragon as a symbol of imperial power.

14: Bronze knife coin
7 CE
A currency known as knife money, based on the scraper knives used by fishermen and nomadic hunters in eastern and northern China, was first used in the fourth century BCE. In the third century BCE, a circular coin with a square hole had replaced knife money. This later coin, from the Wang Mang Period, combines both types. Wang Mang was a powerful figure of the later Western Han Dynasty who then became emperor himself from 9 to 23 CE. He issued twenty-one different types of coins, including this one.

15: Bronze bell
Early fifth century BCE
Music and the harmony it creates were strongly advocated by the great sage Confucius, and there is a long tradition of bells and drums being used to make music for Chinese court ceremonies and rituals. Bells of this kind were imported into the Zhou lands in northern China from the south at the turn of the first millennium BCE. Their new, melodic sounds strongly influenced the rhythm and phrasing of Zhou poetry and writing styles. They were hung as a set, in ascending sizes and timbres, and were played by striking the outside with a hammer. Casting large patterned bells — this one is 15 inches/38.3 centimeters — was a complex and costly process.

16: Gold dagger handle
Sixth to fifth century BCE
This elaborate handle was cast in a mold, using Chinese bronzework techniques. Its fine, fragile design makes it impractical for war. Most likely it was only ever intended for display or perhaps for placement in a tomb. Weapons and warfare were ever-present in ancient China. Rulers needed massive armies of infantrymen and carefully organized logistics to maintain authority over vast territories. This dagger hilt comes from a particularly violent time in the Zhou Dynasty known as the Spring and Autumn Period (770–476 BC). The need for weapons prompted technical advances in iron and steel casting techniques, which had its benefits elsewhere in society, such as the introduction of the iron plow to farming.

Ancient Japan

The archipelago of Japan stretches west toward the Korean peninsula and north toward China. Its Neolithic Period, from 10,000 to 300 BCE, is named Jōmon after a specific type of pottery crafted during this time. The people of this era, also called the Jōmon, were hunter-gatherers who lived mainly in pit dwellings around a central open space.

During the Yayoi Period, from the third century BCE to the third century CE, increased contact with mainland Asia resulted in all types of change. After wet rice agriculture was introduced from Korea and China, there was a shift from hunting and gathering to small farming settlements. Metalworking and other technologies also arrived, and a more structured society emerged. Politically, regional chiefs fought to expand their territories and increase their power.

Burial mounds became the defining feature of the Kofun, or Tumulus, Period, around 300–710 CE. The word *Kofun* means "old mound." During this time, it was common to cover tombs of important people with large, keyhole-shaped mounds of earth. Clan leaders from the Yamato area increased their dominance and became the ruling imperial dynasty. There are no written records until the late Kofun Period, when the Chinese writing system was introduced, alongside Buddhism. With Buddhism came the building of temples, which replaced the mounded tombs of the Kofun Period and ushered in a new cultural era.

Key to plate

17: Earthenware bottle
Around 1500–1000 BCE
Japanese pottery dates back to the beginning of the Jōmon period, around 10,000 BCE, making it among the oldest in the world. Jōmon means "cord-marked." Pots, bowls, and bottles were shaped from coils of clay, decorated with markings from cord, then fired in an outdoor bonfire. This bottle comes from the northern Honshu area in the late Jōmon Period. It is relatively small and simple in design, with thin walls that indicate an improvement in technique from the early and mid-Jōmon Periods. Its abstract decoration is an indigenous Japanese style, typical of the northern region.

18: Kofun tomb figure
Sixth century CE
This unglazed, hollow terra-cotta figure would have been one of hundreds of sculptures placed on and around a tomb mound. The sculptures are tomb guardians, called *haniwa*, and were first introduced in the early Kofun Period as simple cylindrical forms. The size of the tomb mound and the number of *haniwa* needed to protect it reflected the power and status of the deceased. An emperor's tomb could be several hundred yards/meters across, with thousands of *haniwa*. Figures such as this seated woman are thought to symbolize continued service to the deceased in the afterlife. They varied in height from 1 to 5 feet/ 30 to 150 centimeters. This figure is 27 inches/68.5 centimeters high and reveals the typical clothing for women at that time. The wraparound garment, the jewelry on the neck, wrists, and ankles, and the use of combs to create an elaborate hairstyle are all shown in detail.

19: Bronze Buddha
Eighth century CE
Buddhism and Buddhist art arrived in Japan from mainland Asia in the Kofun Period. This Buddha statue is of the Yakushi (medicine) Buddha, who can grant relief from illnesses. His upturned left hand would have held a medicine pot, and his raised right hand was a gesture meaning "no fear." This statue is very similar to Tang Dynasty statues of the Buddha from mainland China, indicating that it was strongly influenced by Chinese culture. Buddhism and Confucianism were introduced to Japan in the sixth century CE, but the Japanese already had a system of religious beliefs and practices. They worshipped many deities and saw divine power in nature as well as in the acts of great men. Their belief system had no founder, no religious texts, and originally no name, until it became necessary to distinguish it from Buddhism, when it was called Shinto. The guiding beliefs of Shintoism continue to inform Japan's culture as do Buddhism, Taoism, and Confucianism. Buddhism remained the dominant influence on Japanese art until the tenth century CE.

17

18

19

Ancient Korea

The kingdom of Silla was one of three ancient kingdoms on the Korean peninsula. Founded in 57 BCE, it gradually grew in strength, wealth, and dominion, annexing other parts of the peninsula and eventually taking control of the other two dominant kingdoms, the Koguryo and the Paekche, in 668 CE. The Unified Silla Dynasty then lasted from 668 to 935 CE. Its capital, Gyeongju, meaning "city of gold," was one of the great cities of the ancient world.

There are many similarities between the Silla era and the Kofun Period in Japan, including a tradition of mounding earth over large tombs holding sumptuous treasures. Painted scenes inside the Sillan tombs reveal how the rich lived — hunting, feasting, and enjoying music and dancing. Tomb goods showcase skilled work in ceramics, bronze, and, in particular, gold. They also reveal contact with foreign cultures, including the nomadic horse-riding tribes of central Asia. Sillan tombs include objects from as far away as the Mediterranean.

The Sillas' main outside influence was China, which even had a colony to the north of the Korean kingdoms from 108 BCE to 313 CE and continued to have contact with the peninsula thereafter. The introduction of Buddhism from 372 CE onward had a profound effect on Silla culture. Buddhism was adopted as its official religion in the sixth century CE, and the Silla rulers became generous patrons of Buddhist art.

Key to plate

20: Gold crown

Fifth century CE

This crown comes from the north mound of a great double tomb known as Hwangnam Daechong. A king was buried under the south mound and his queen under the north. Silla tombs were wooden and built above ground, sealed with clay, then topped with mounds of stone and earth. As a result, they were largely impenetrable and their treasures have been protected until relatively recently. Extraordinary jewelry, pottery, and metal vessels have been discovered in the tombs, as well as gold and silver regalia. The most elaborate tombs come from the fifth and sixth centuries CE, before Buddhism's influence took hold. The design of this gold crown, with its carved jade ornaments, most likely resulted from contact with the nomadic peoples of central Asia, as well as the Chinese.

21: House-shaped funeral urn

Eighth century CE

After the rise of Buddhism, massive tomb mounds fell out of favor as the Silla adopted the practice of cremation. The designs on the urns holding the ashes of the deceased give useful insight into life at the time. This earthenware urn follows the design of a grand Silla house from the eighth century, with a complex tiled roof. The hollow house model would have contained an inner urn to hold the ashes and doors on hinges to cover the opening. The choice of a domestic house to hold the ashes suggests a wish for a comfortable existence in the next life.

22: Iron horse armor

Fifth century CE

This piece of armor, known as a chanfron, was used to protect a horse's head in battle. It is evidence of the military strength of the wealthy Silla kingdom. Tomb paintings from this period show warriors on horseback, with both horse and rider covered in armor. Iron armor was first made in Korea in the fourth century CE as conflict escalated among the Koguryo, Paekche, and Silla kingdoms. The skill and resources needed to manufacture the armor meant it would only have been available to those with power and wealth.

23: Gilt bronze *bodhisattva* statue

Late sixth to early seventh century CE

A *bodhisattva* was originally a portrayal of the Buddha in one of his previous lives, before he reached enlightenment. It later became the name for anyone on the way to enlightenment. As such, the *bodhisattvas* were seen as accessible manifestations of the Buddha and were particularly popular in Korea and Japan. This statue of a *bodhisattva* is shown in what is known as the pensive pose. It is strongly influenced by Chinese Buddhist art, which, in turn, took its inspiration from India. A striking example of how Buddhism changed the Silla kingdom is the use of gold here for decorating religious ornaments, rather than for personal adornment or grave goods.

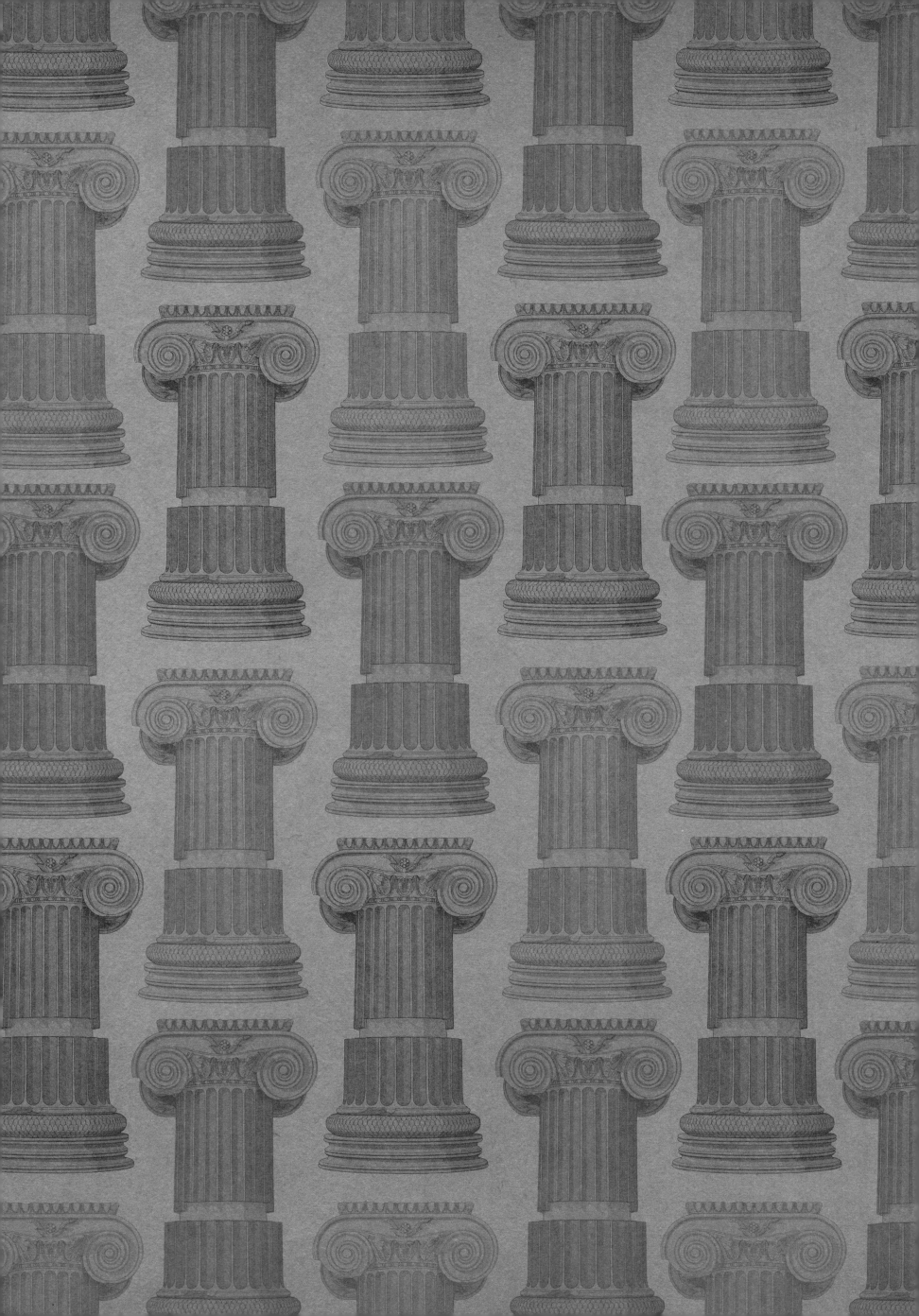

HISTORIUM

Gallery 4

Europe

The Celts

Ancient Greece

Ancient Rome

The Vikings

The Celts

Over two thousand years ago, Europe north of the Mediterranean was dominated by many different Iron Age tribes and ethnic groups, including the Gauls, Britons, and Gaels. Today these different groups of people are often referred to collectively as the Celts. Famed for being fearsome warriors, the Celts were also farmers, merchants, miners, and highly skilled artisans.

Their laws, myths, and beliefs were passed on orally by druids and bards. Much of what we know about the Celts comes from accounts written by the Greeks and Romans and from the elaborately decorated objects that the Celts themselves left behind. Celtic art and religion were strongly informed by the natural world. The Celts took patterns from nature and stylized them in abstract, swirling lines. From 500 BCE to 100 CE, this art style spread across trade routes from Ireland to Romania. It is now known as La Tène art, after an area in Switzerland where many objects have been found.

From the fourth to the first centuries BCE, the Celts came into direct conflict with the Romans and Greeks. At first, the Celts were often victorious in battle, but the increasing might of the Roman armies and the expanding Germanic tribes forced Celtic culture into decline. A final flourish of Celtic-style art came from the Celtic Christians of Ireland and Britain in the seventh and eighth centuries CE. Their gradual conversion to Christianity had enabled them to incorporate elements of Celtic culture into their new faith.

Key to plate

1: The Battersea Shield
350–50 BCE

Many Celtic cultures lavished their artistic skill on weapons. Warfare was a dominant feature of Celtic life, and warriors were highly respected. This shield is too short and elaborate to have been made for battle. With its polished bronze and prominent red enamel studs, it was probably made for display. Its place of discovery, in the Thames River at Battersea, London, suggests it may have been a religious offering.

2: Agris parade helmet
Around 350 BCE

Parade helmets, usually associated with ancient Gaul specifically, are a striking symbol of Celtic warrior culture. The skillful metalwork on this helmet is typical of the early La Tène style and shows strong Mediterranean influences. Discovered in a cave in France, the helmet appears to have been a ritual offering to the spirits of the underworld. The Celts believed that boundaries between the supernatural and real worlds were weaker at certain times and places and that both the living and the dead were able to pass through them. Offerings

of this quality and value show how greatly the Celts revered — and feared — their deities.

3: The Great Torc of Snettisham
75 BCE

A torc is a heavy gold or silver ring that was worn around the neck in some Celtic cultures. Celtic deities are depicted wearing them, Celtic warriors are described in battle as naked except for their weapons and torcs, and the famous warrior queen Boudicca is said to have worn one. As well as being a display of wealth and status, the torc was probably worn as an amulet to protect its wearer from harm. This torc is part of an incredible treasure hoard found buried in a field in Snettisham, England. It is made from sixty-four threads of gold mixed with silver, twisted with a craftsmanship and complexity that surpasses the metalwork of other civilizations at that time.

4: Gundestrup cauldron
First century BCE

This silver cauldron was found in a bog in Denmark. The plates it was made from had been carefully taken

apart, and the cauldron was then left, presumably as a gift to the gods. Cauldrons were prestigious objects in Celtic times, widely used for rituals, as well as for cooking and serving food. The scenes on this cauldron combine familiar Celtic imagery with unknown gods and unusual animals, in a style that is more common to a group known as the Thracians. This cauldron could have been a gift to a Celtic chief, war booty, or even a collaboration between tribes.

5: The Lindisfarne Gospels
Around 700 CE

Lindisfarne was a monastic community on England's northeast coast. It was founded in 634 CE by Irish monks. The Irish Celts, or Gaels, had managed to assimilate facets of Celtic culture into Christian worship. The Lindisfarne Gospels give stunning examples of this fusion. The book's illuminated text is the work of a single artist, possibly a bishop or abbot. Each gospel begins with sumptuously decorated pages, combining swirling symbols from Celtic metalwork with Mediterranean and Anglo-Saxon elements in a style known as insular art.

Ancient Greece

Ancient Greece consisted of several hundred self-governing city-states, sprinkled around the mainland coast and on islands in the Mediterranean Sea. They began to emerge in 800 BCE, each with its own ruler, army, laws, and coins. Surrounded by sea, the ancient Greeks became great travelers and traders, exporting their culture to distant shores as well as bringing back influences from Egypt and the Near East.

The Greeks worshipped a host of gods and goddesses, each one representing a different aspect of everyday life. There was a stronger emphasis on the physical world than the afterlife, although proper burial rituals were considered essential. People honored the gods by demonstrating physical fitness in sporting events, holding grand processions, and presenting gifts or sacrifices at temples. They hoped the gods in turn would answer their prayers for health and good fortune.

As the city-states flourished, the Greeks developed their own alphabet, followed by a wealth of poetry, drama, sculpture, painting, and philosophy. In 338 BCE, the Macedonian king Philip II invaded, and for the first time, all of Greece came under the rule of one person. Philip's son, Alexander the Great, opened up trade routes with the East, spread Greek culture as far as India and Egypt, and brought back new riches and influences. After his death, Greece gradually became fragmented again, and by the second century BCE, its power was on the wane. The Romans invaded in 146 BCE, and Greece became part of the Roman Empire.

6

7

6: Bronze figure of a running girl
Around 520–500 BCE
This bronze figure, only 4½ inches/ 11.4 centimeters high, was probably made in Sparta, a city-state known for its bronze figures as well as its warriors and athletes. In most city-states, women were not citizens, but the Spartans encouraged girls to exercise and take part in competitions. Their oldest and most famous sporting event was the Olympic Games, held every four years in the Spartan city of Olympia. In the fourth century BCE, a Spartan princess, Kyniska, won several chariot races.

7: Marble temple column
Early third century BCE
This column is from the Temple of Artemis at Sardis. Only the top and lower section are shown here. The original would have been 59 feet/ 18 meters tall and formed part of a majestic building eight columns wide and twenty columns long. Gods and goddesses were an integral part of Greek culture, and every city-state had at least one temple built in their honor.

8: Gold-glass *alabastron*
First century BCE
Perfume was an important commodity in the ancient world. Small vessels like this one were designed to hold perfumed oils. Perfume was used in the burial of the dead, the worship of gods, for medicinal purposes, or simply for personal use as a symbol of status.

9: Gold goat-head earrings
200–100 BCE
The fashion for gold jewelry exploded after Alexander the Great conquered the Persian Empire in 331 BCE and vast quantities of gold became available to the Greeks. Animal heads were popular motifs on earrings, and wild goats were particularly favored. The intricate designs showed off both the technical expertise of the artist and the wealth of the wearer. These goats' eyes are set with garnets, possibly from India.

10: *Dinos* (mixing bowl)
Seventh century BCE
Many wonderful examples of Greek pottery have survived to this day. The pale clay background color of this bowl is typical of the Corinth area. It is painted with goats, panthers, lions, and mythical sphinxes. This bowl would have been used to mix water and wine. Winemaking was a major part of Greek life. There was even a god, Dionysus, who oversaw the process.

11

12

13

14

Key to plate

11: Dying Warrior sculpture
Around 480 BCE
This is one of a group of sculptures depicting battle between the Greeks and Trojans. The sculptures once stood on the east pediment—the gable above the colonnades—of the Temple of Aphaia on the island of Aigina. This sculpture depicts a warrior struggling to rise from the ground, his emotions evident in his face and body position. Earlier figures in Greek art were more rigid, forward-facing, and staged. This statue is an example of the classical style, with its naturalism and strong focus on the human form, which was just beginning when this temple was built.

12: Fragment from the Parthenon
Around 438–432 BCE
Still visible in modern-day Athens, the Parthenon is the most famous of the ancient buildings in the Acropolis. This fragment is part of a 525-foot-/

160-meter-long frieze from the outside wall of the Parthenon. It depicts the procession that took place in the city every year as part of a festival in honor of the goddess Athena. In this scene, a cow is being led to the temple altar for sacrifice. Blood sacrifices lay at the heart of Greek religious rituals. Athena was the goddess of war, and since city-states were often fighting one another, people would make a considerable effort to have her on their side.

13: Black-figured amphora
Around 530–520 BCE
The ancient Greeks also revered heroes like those found in Homer's epic poems, the *Iliad* and the *Odyssey*, which were composed between 750 and 650 BCE. The poems provided a rich source of imagery for Greek art. The painting on this wine jar shows a scene from the *Iliad*, in which the warrior hero Achilles kills the Amazon

queen Penthesilea. This amphora was made in Athens and is signed by the potter Exekias, who most likely painted it as well. Exekias depicted black figures on a clay background—called the black-figure technique—which prevailed in the early sixth century BCE.

14: Red-figured *psykter*
Around 520–510 BCE
Around 530 BCE, a new pottery painting style known as the red-figure technique emerged. Instead of showing figures in black against a clay background, artists painted the background black, leaving the figures as red clay with some added brushwork. This vase for cooling wine shows young male athletes and their trainers in a gymnasium. The athletes are nude, as was the custom for male competitors. We can see an athlete preparing to throw the javelin. His name, Batrachos, is inscribed beside him.

Ancient Rome

According to legend, Rome was founded in 753 BCE by its first king, Romulus, who with his brother, Remus, was nursed by a she-wolf when the two were abandoned as infants. Archaeological remains date the first settlement of Rome to the ninth century BCE. By 246 BCE, Rome had conquered the entire Italian peninsula, and at its height, in 117 CE, the Roman Empire encompassed lands as far north as Britain and as far south as Egypt.

The Roman army was a highly structured fighting force and was responsible for the empire's vast conquests. Professional soldiers served for twenty-five years or more and could look forward to pensions and gifts of land at the end of their service.

The Romans were heavily influenced by Greek culture; they studied and imitated Greek art, religion, and science. Perhaps the empire's greatest achievements came from Roman engineers, who built enormous buildings and networks of roads and waterways unlike anything the world had seen before. This building, as well as many aspects of farming and civic life, were made possible by a vast number of slaves held captive by the empire.

Religion was important to the Romans, and for most of its history, magnificent temples throughout the empire were devoted to many different gods. In 380 CE, Rome adopted Christianity as its sole religion. During the fifth and sixth centuries CE, the empire lost control of its western provinces and the city of Rome was sacked by Germanic tribes. The eastern Roman Empire survived for another thousand years until its capital, Constantinople, was sacked in 1453 CE.

Key to plate

15: **Augustus of Prima Porta**
First century BCE
This statue of the Roman emperor Augustus was discovered in 1863 in a suburb of Rome called Prima Porta. Augustus, who was born Octavian, was Rome's first emperor.

Until the first century BCE, Rome was a republic, ruled by a senate of prominent citizens, but in 45 BCE, Octavian's great-uncle, Julius Caesar, became the sole ruler of Rome. While Julius Caesar never called himself emperor, he became supreme dictator. This angered the senators, and in 44 BCE, Caesar was murdered by a group of them. Between 43 and 33 BCE, Rome was ruled by three men, Marc Antony, Marcus Aemilius Lepidus, and Octavian, in a union called the Second Triumvirate, but this arrangement

dissolved into civil war. Octavian emerged victorious and took the name Augustus Caesar when he became emperor of Rome in 27 BCE.

Augustus needed to establish his authority in all of the empire's far-flung corners. One way of doing this was to make sure his image was ever present. Many images of Augustus survive. Statues were erected all over the empire, and images of the emperor's head also appeared on coins.

This statue shows Augustus as a young man with the traditional proportions of an Athenian athlete. The image of eternal youth was a classical Greek ideal, and no images of Augustus have been found showing him as an older man.

The statue also depicts Augustus as a strong military leader, wearing

an ornate breastplate. The statue of Cupid at his feet could be to remind viewers that the emperor is semi-divine; Augustus claimed to be descended from the goddess Venus, Cupid's mother.

After Augustus's death, in 14 CE, the senate pronounced him a god, and his image continued to be used as a symbol of imperial power. This statue dates from that era and is believed to have been commissioned by Augustus's adopted son, Tiberius, who became the second emperor of Rome.

Throughout the Roman Empire, emperors would commission likenesses of themselves as symbols of power. The emperor Nero (37–68 CE) even had a 9-foot-/3-meter-high bronze statue of himself made. Rome's famous Colosseum is named after this colossus.

15

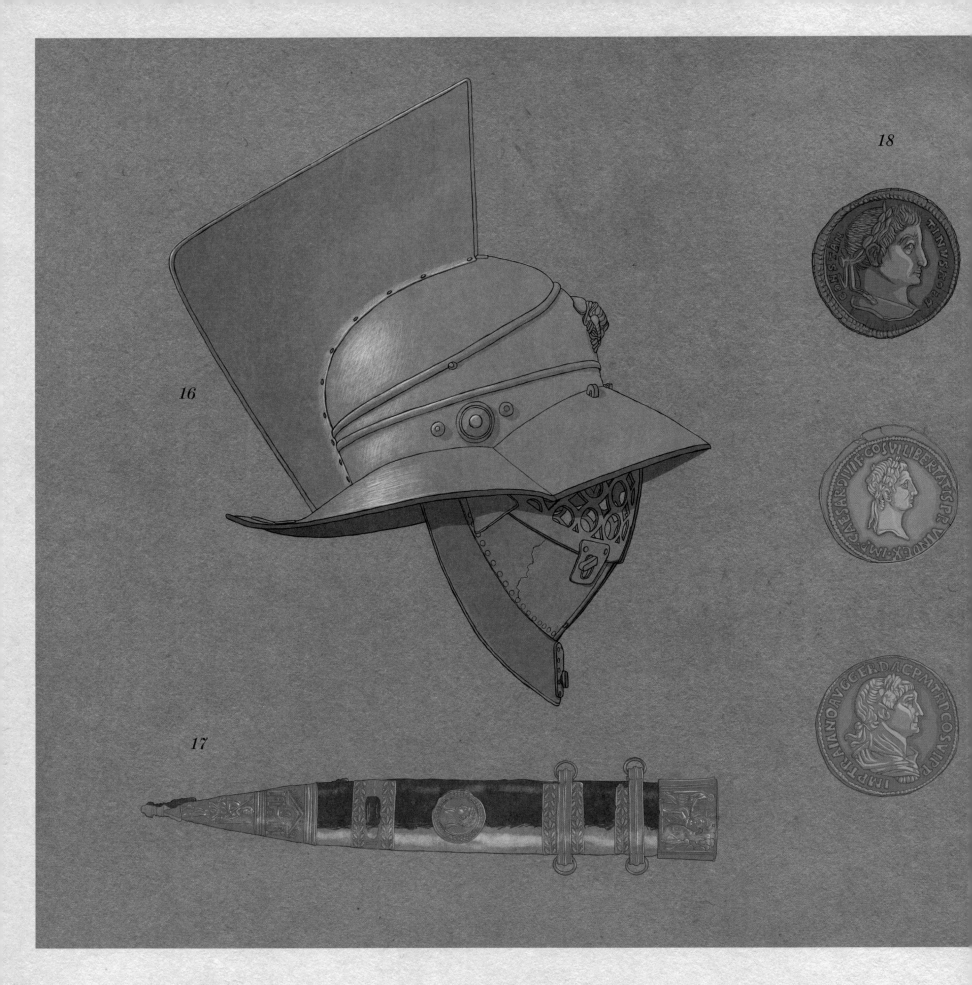

16

17

Key to plate

16: Gladiator's helmet
First century CE
This helmet would have been worn by a Roman gladiator. The gladiators would fight in Roman arenas such as the Colosseum for the entertainment of the Roman people. These were usually battles to the death. Gladiatorial tournaments would be paid for by emperors or powerful citizens wanting to gain the favor of the masses. Many gladiators were slaves, and it was a gladiator,

Spartacus, who led an uprising of Roman slaves in the first century BCE.

17: The sword of Tiberius
First century CE
This sword and scabbard, probably commissioned by a senior officer of the Roman army, is decorated with a bronze image of the emperor Tiberius. That it was found in Mainz, Germany, shows how far the Roman legions traveled during military duty. This prestigious, decorated item was

probably made to celebrate victory after a long campaign in Germany. Roman legionaries had to be Roman citizens and would serve for twenty-five years. Legionaries carried two javelins, a sword, a dagger, and a shield. The Roman legions were rigorously trained and fought in formation.

18: Roman coins
First, second, and fourth centuries CE
These three coins show the Roman emperors Augustus, Trajan, and

19

Constantine the Great. Roman coins were minted in both Rome and various parts of the Roman Empire: the coin showing Constantine, for instance, was minted in Germany. The image of an emperor's head on coinage was another way of establishing the ruler's presence throughout the empire. Trajan was a successful general, and Trajan's column, which stands in Rome today, is still a dramatic reminder of his victory over a people called the Dacians.

Constantine is best known as the first Christian emperor of Rome.

19: Fresco from Pompeii
First century CE

Roman women were expected to be wives and mothers and had very little political or social power. Some very wealthy women, however, were well educated and managed to exert significant political influence. This wall painting shows a young woman holding a stylus (an implement for writing in soft wax) to her lips and holding a *polyptych* (a book of wax tablets). The ability to write was a symbol of status in ancient Rome. The city of Pompeii was buried by ash in 79 CE when Mount Vesuvius erupted. Many important Roman artifacts have been discovered buried in the ash.

20

21

22

—— *Key to plate* ——

20: Water spout
First century CE
This terra-cotta water spout in the shape of a lion would have formed only a tiny part of the intricate network of waterways in ancient Rome. Roman engineers built enormous aqueducts that carried fresh water into cities; one example still standing is the Pont du Gard, in France, which dates from the first century CE. Only very wealthy Romans had running water in their homes, but poor citizens could get clean water from public fountains, and there were even public toilets with flowing water to carry waste away. Eventually, eleven aqueducts were built to carry water to the city of Rome.

21: Statue of Jupiter
Second century CE
This bronze statue shows the chief of the Roman gods, Jupiter (known as Zeus to the Greeks). The Romans endowed their local gods with the personalities of the much more lively Greek pantheon, and this statue may be a copy of a Greek original. It is impossible to say how many gods the ancient Romans worshipped because as well as the famous gods of Mount Olympus, most Roman households had their own guardian spirits.

22: The Portland Vase
Around 5–25 CE
The Portland Vase is an accomplished example of Roman cameo-glass, which demonstrates the sophistication of Roman glassblowing. Cameo-glass vessels would have been difficult to make, as the technique required that two different-colored glasses were fused together and that the top layer was carved and polished. Cameo-glass was produced only briefly in Rome, and surviving examples nearly all date from between 27 BCE and 68 CE.

Glassblowing was invented in the first century BCE, and the technique meant that large vessels for everyday use could be made in great numbers for the first time. It also meant that the creation of larger luxury vessels was possible. Prior to the discovery of glassblowing, glass production had been restricted to small luxury items.

23 (opposite page): Mosaic
Second century CE
Wealthy Roman houses were lavishly decorated, and floors were often covered in intricate mosaics. This example was found in Pompeii; it shows detailed images of the sort of Mediterranean seafood that Roman diners would have enjoyed. Banqueting was an important social ritual for wealthy Romans, and rare, expensive foods were served to impress.

24

25

26

27

28

The Vikings

The Vikings are best known for their daring raids by sea and their sagas detailing heroic battles. It was a raid on the monastery of Lindisfarne, on the English coast, that marked the beginning of the Viking Age in 793 CE. Most Vikings were content to stay at home in Scandinavia, farming and trading. The Viking raiders formed only a tiny minority of the Scandinavian people, yet it was their audacity that gave the Viking Age its identity.

The early Vikings were great traders and travelers. Their journeys revealed the rich pickings to be had in foreign places, and soon trading turned into raiding. The success of Viking raids owed much to their superior ship technology. No one could beat Viking ships for speed, and none of the kingdoms they attacked had large enough armies to stop them.

At first the raids were hit-and-run attacks. Next, raiders decided to overwinter on foreign shores. Finally, they started settling abroad permanently. The Vikings continued to search for new territories and would eventually have settlements in Russia, the Scottish Islands, Ireland, Iceland, and Greenland.

Viking travelers brought with them a passion and flair for display, both in their distinctive interweaving patterns and in their love of precious metals. Above all, they brought a bloodthirsty determination and a fierce warrior culture.

The Viking Age began with an attack on Christianity and ended some four hundred years later with an acceptance of that religion. The cultural changes brought by this new faith, as well as the centralization of European kingdoms, brought an end to the Viking Age.

Key to plate

24: Cup from the Vale of York hoard

Ninth century CE

This silver cup is the largest, most spectacular object in the Vale of York hoard. Most of the other objects, including 617 coins, were found inside it. The objects came from as far afield as Afghanistan, Russia, and Ireland, showing how widely the Vikings raided and traded. The cup, inscribed with vines and hunting scenes, was probably made in northern France or Germany in the mid-ninth century CE. It may well have been looted from a wealthy monastery.

25: Ship brooch

800–1050 CE

This copper brooch would have been used to fasten a Viking's thick woolen cloak at the shoulder. Its detailed design demonstrates the Vikings' skill in metalwork as well as their passion for display. The Vikings were rightly proud of their sleek, swift longships, which cut through oceans and glided up rivers. This brooch shows animal heads shaped into the fore and aft stems of the ship. It was common for ships to be elaborately decorated, in order to make a striking impression as they sped toward a foreign shore.

26: Silver-inlaid ax head

Tenth century CE

Viking culture glorified courageous, powerful warriors. Young men would rally to fight for successful warrior leaders. Vikings were fearsome in battle and excelled in hand-to-hand combat. Men who died on the battlefield were thought to enjoy a lavish, exciting afterlife in Valhalla, the great hall of the underworld. Axes were common Viking weapons. The longsword and the spear were seen as superior, but the silver patterning on this ax marks it out as a treasured possession.

27: The Lewis Chessmen

1150–1200 CE

Chess was a popular game across Europe in the twelfth century CE. These pieces, carved out of walrus ivory and whales' teeth, were found in the Isle of Lewis, off the northwest coast of Scotland. It is likely that the chess pieces belonged to a Norwegian merchant traveling from Norway to Ireland. Of particular interest are the pieces in the shape of warders, which take the place of modern-day rooks. They are based on mythical Viking warriors who, according to the Viking sagas, worked themselves into a frenzy before fighting, then ran onto the battlefield with their eyes rolling and biting on their shields. Interestingly, these warriors carry shields decorated with a Christian cross. Christian missionaries had been present in Scandinavia from the ninth century CE, but conversion was gradual.

28: Coins from the Vale of York hoard

927 CE

Coins were a relatively late addition to the Viking economy. Early Viking traders would travel south to exchange furs, weapons, and slaves for Arabian silver coins. It was the silver content they were interested in, though, not the coins themselves. Back home the Vikings melted the coins down and used the silver to create other items. Silver neck and arm rings were made of standard weights so they could double as currency or be hacked into smaller weights. When the Vikings settled in England, they copied the local custom and began minting their own coins. These coins were found in a hoard near the important Viking town of Jorvik (modern York).

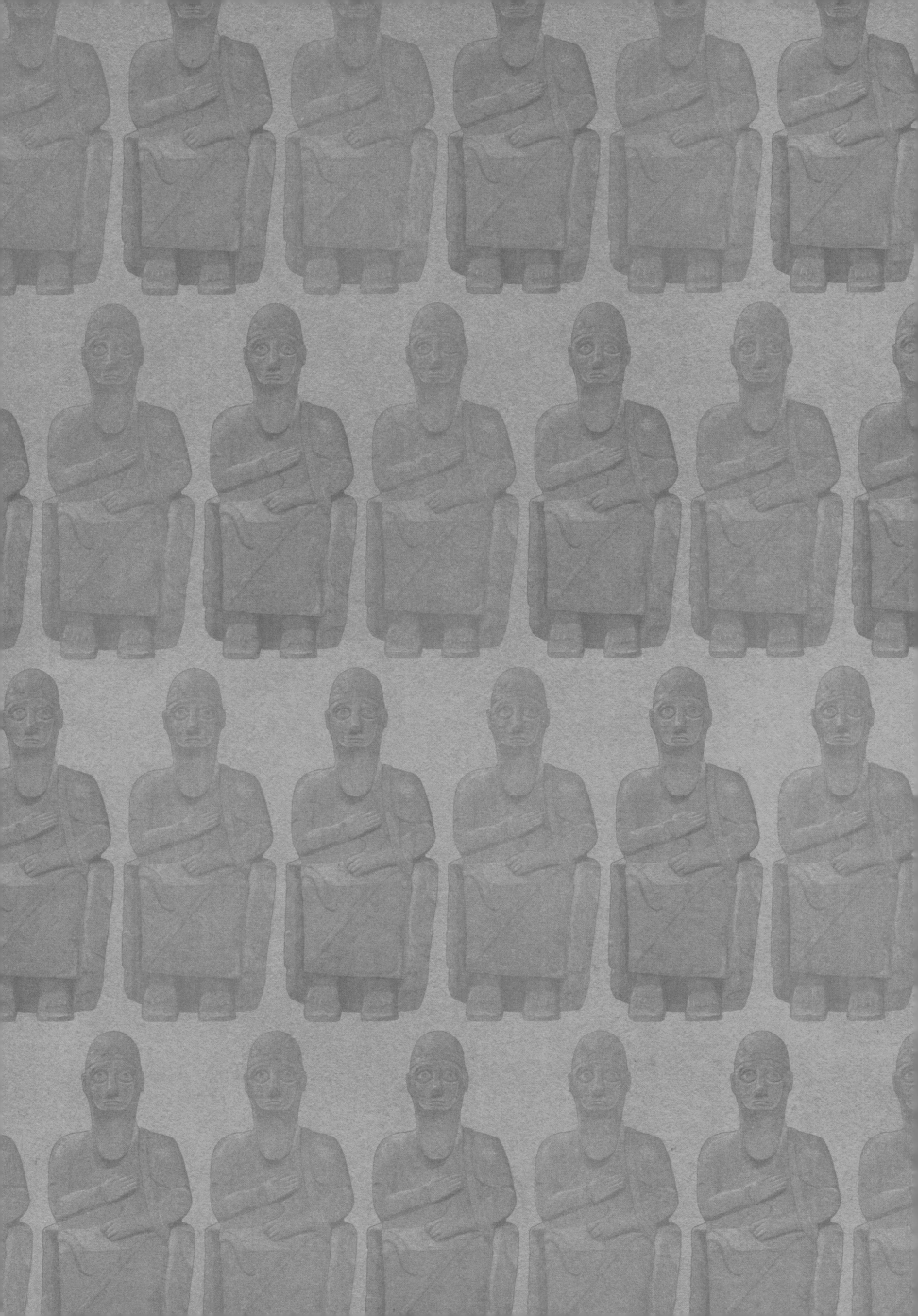

Gallery 5

The Middle East

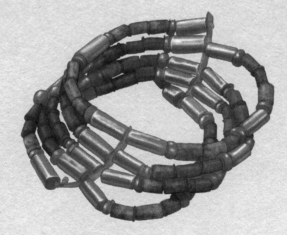

Mesopotamia
The Ancient Levant
Ancient Persia
Early Islam

Mesopotamia

Mesopotamia was located around the Tigris and Euphrates Rivers in land encompassed by modern-day Syria, Iraq, Iran, Turkey, and Kuwait. Archaeological evidence suggests that it was the birthplace of the first cities, the first system of writing, and the earliest known written laws, in addition to the place where the wheel, the sailing boat, the seed plow, and even the measurement of time in hours, minutes, and seconds were invented. Such innovation was made possible by Mesopotamia's location. The rich soil deposited by the rivers surrounding the area enabled farmers to grow surplus produce that fed expanding urban populations.

Ancient Mesopotamia was not one unified culture, but rather multiple civilizations whose influence waxed and waned over thousands of years. Notable Mesopotamian civilizations include the Sumerians, the Akkadians, the Babylonians, and the Assyrians. These people spoke different languages and competed for power but learned from one another's cultures and shared beliefs in a multitude of gods. The threat of war was ever present, but the prospect of trade was often more attractive—especially in the south, where there were few natural resources.

The emergence of cities, like the city of Ur (in what is now Iraq), began in the Copper Age around 4500 BCE with the Sumerians. By the Middle Bronze Age—around 2000 BCE—the Assyrian kingdom in the north had expanded and the city of Babylon had risen to prominence. Invasions from forces outside Mesopotamia, such as the Kassites and the Hittites, weakened these kingdoms, but despite those attacks, newly consolidated Assyrian and Babylonian empires existed in the Iron Age (1000–500 BCE).

Around 500 BCE, indigenous Mesopotamian cultures experienced decline as foreign powers became increasingly dominant: first the Persians, next the Greeks, then the Romans. The Arab conquest of Mesopotamia in the seventh century CE led to the spread of Islam throughout the region.

Key to plate

1: **Royal cemetery, Ur: Standard of Ur**
Around 2600–2500 BCE
This wooden box, inlaid with mosaic, is a work of art from the Sumerian period. It was described as a plaque by Leonard Woolley, the archaeologist who discovered it in the 1920s, but its purpose is unknown. It is 23 inches/ 58 centimeters long and decorated on all sides with shells, lapis lazuli, and red marble. On the side shown here, the agricultural roots of Sumerian wealth are clearly depicted. In the lower two strips, produce is being brought as a tribute, while in the top strip, the king and other members of the elite are feasting. The other side of the box shows the Sumerian army—a representation of the force necessary to defend the kingdom.

2: **Royal cemetery, Ur: headdress**
Around 2600–2500 BCE
This circlet of gold beech leaves was found on the head of a female attendant in the royal cemetery of Ur. The leaves are separated by beads of lapis lazuli and carnelian. In total, sixteen grand tombs were found in the center of the cemetery. The rulers buried here seem to predate the first recorded dynasty of Ur, since their names do not appear on the list of Sumerian kings. It is possible that they were local rulers, which makes the wealth of their tomb goods all the more astonishing.

3: **Royal cemetery, Ur: gold cup**
Around 2600–2500 BCE
There were no precious metals to be found in the flat floodplains of southern Mesopotamia. The gold used to make this cup probably came from the Elam, who lived in what is now Iran, or the Hattians, from Anatolia (modern Turkey). It would have been created by skilled local artisans for the ruling elite. The Mesopotamians believed that the souls of the dead were doomed to dwell in a dismal underworld. These goods may have been an attempt to make the afterlife less bleak. It is also possible that the items were intended as gifts for the deities, particularly the queen of the underworld, Ereshkigal.

4: **Royal cemetery, Ur: statuette**
Around 2600–2500 BCE
Crafted out of wood and decorated primarily with gold leaf and shell, this statuette shows a goat on its hind legs reaching to eat leaves from a tree. Land for grazing animals and fertile soil for crops were essential elements of Ur's success.

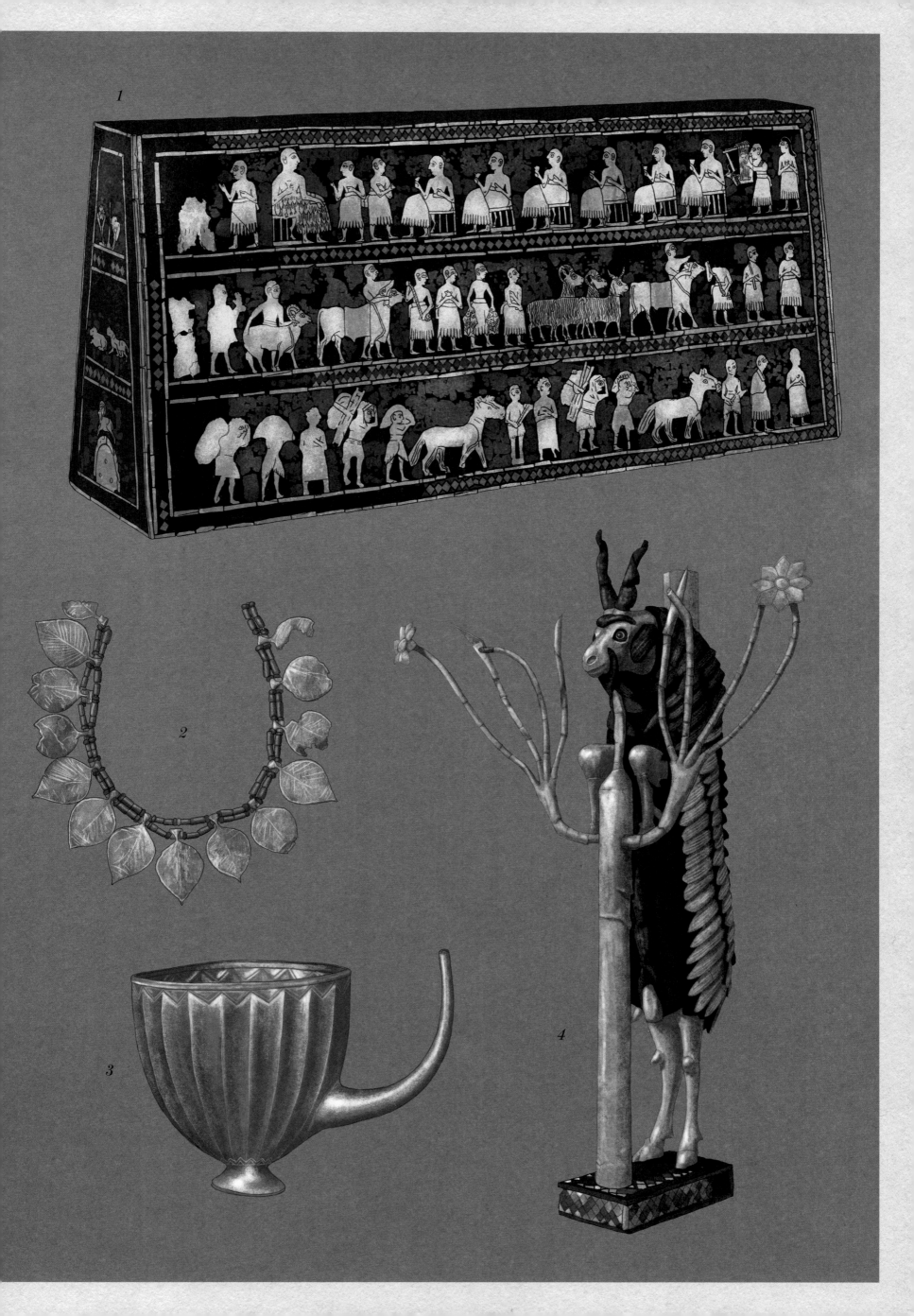

1

2

3

4

Key to plate

5: Royal cemetery, Ur: board game
Around 2600–2500 BCE
Examples of board games with twenty squares have been found from the eastern Mediterranean and Egypt across to India and date from 3000 BCE to the first millennium CE. This board and several similar ones, some still with their gaming pieces were found in the tombs at Ur. Like the Standard of Ur, the wooden boards are beautifully inlaid with lapis lazuli, shell, and red limestone. The inclusion of board games among burial goods suggests that the people of Ur may have expected everyday activities to continue in the afterlife.

6: Head of a ruler
Around 2300–2000 BCE
This heavy bronze head comes from the Early Bronze Age in Mesopotamia, probably from the time of the Akkadian Empire (2334–2150 BCE). The attention to facial detail suggests that it is a true portrait of a king. The Akkadian kings were based at the city-state of Akkad (thought to have been near modern Baghdad). Much of their art was created to glorify their power in southern Mesopotamia. Akkadian people spoke a different language from the Sumerians,

but the two kingdoms were closely linked culturally and politically.

7: Sumerian statue
Around 2900–2600 BCE
Many statues like this one have been discovered on the site of ancient Sumerian temples. They all have similar poses of reverence, with clasped hands and wide-open eyes. This one was found in the ancient Sumerian (later Akkadian) city of Eshnunna, north of Babylon. In the center of every Sumerian city there was a temple that contained a sacred shrine to the city's patron deity. Only priests would have had regular access to the shrine, and it is thought that these statues were taken to the shrine as representatives of worshippers who could not be there in person. This statue may depict a priest, since it does not have the full beard and long hair typical in Mesopotamian images of men.

8: Royal cemetery, Ur: seal
2600–2500 BCE
Around 4000 BCE, the Sumerians began using personal seals to mark ownership, prevent tampering, and as a sort of signature. Cylinder-shaped

seals—hollow tubes of stone or terra-cotta that left a unique pattern when rolled in soft clay—soon emerged. The green cylinder seal here bears the pattern of a banquet scene, as seen in the accompanying clay impression. Many such banquet-scene seals have been found in the tombs of women, whereas combat scenes are more commonly found in the tombs of men.

9: Lion-hunting panel
883–859 BCE
This alabaster relief comes from the Assyrian city of Nimrud (also called Kalhu), to the north of Mesopotamia, in modern Iraq. The Assyrian kings lined their mud-brick palace walls with stone panels depicting their triumphs. This tradition was initiated by King Ashurnasirpal II, shown here aiming his bow at a lion. Hunting lions was a sport associated with kings, since it symbolized their role as fighters and defenders of the people. Ashurnasirpal II was a ruthless monarch who led many successful campaigns that contributed to the establishment of the Neo-Assyrian Empire, which began around 911 BCE and lasted until 609 BCE.

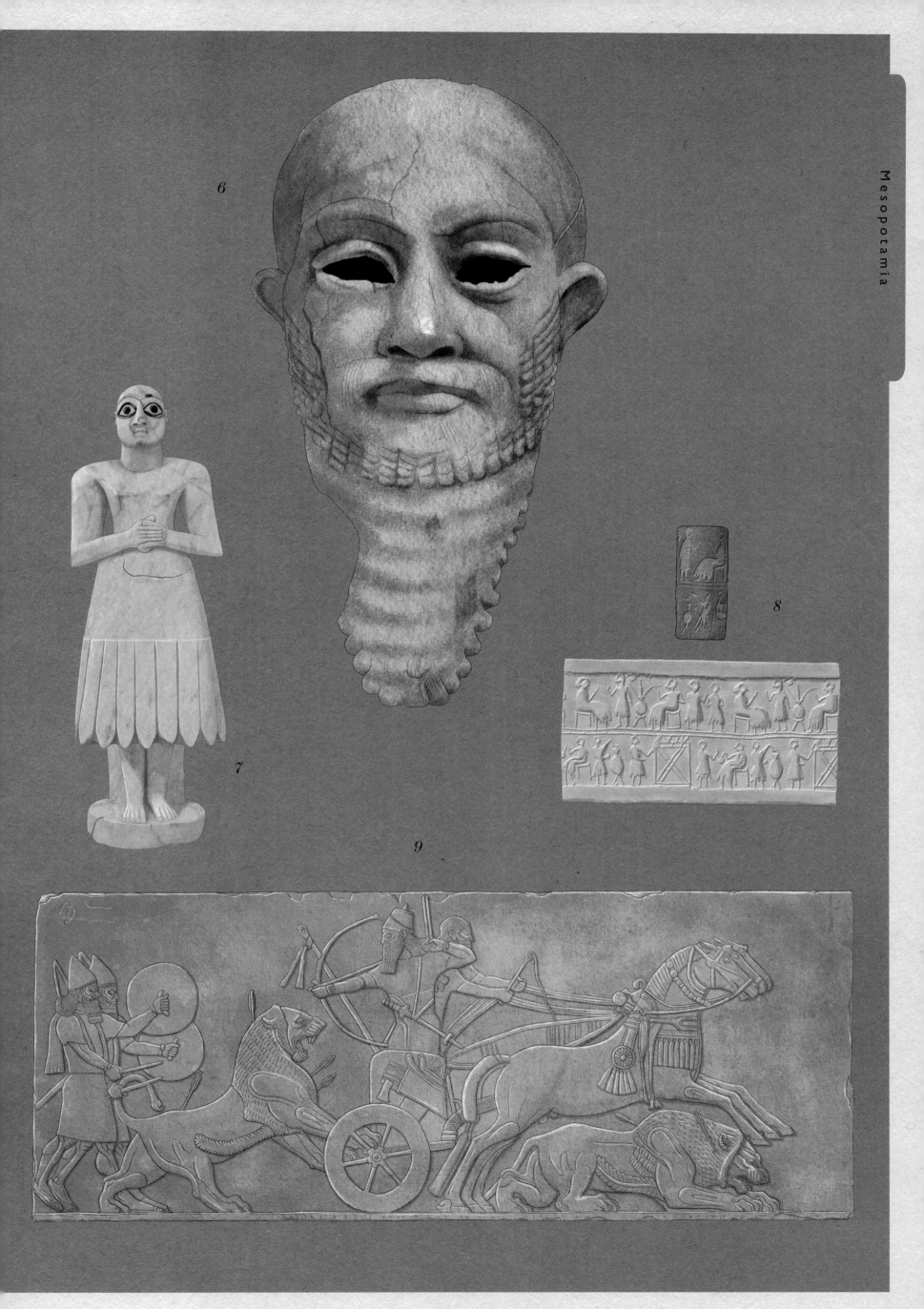

6

7

8

9

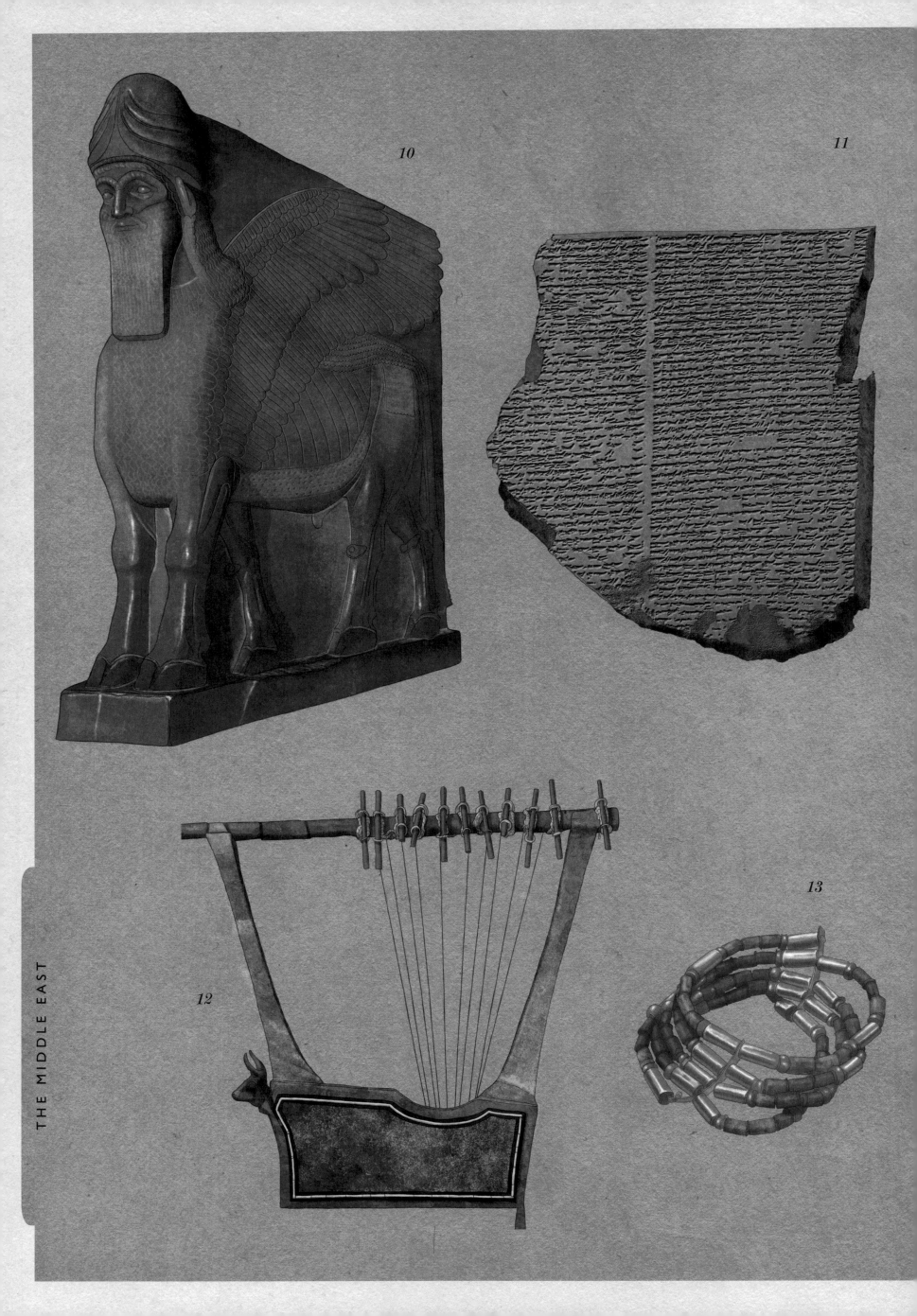

10

11

12

13

14

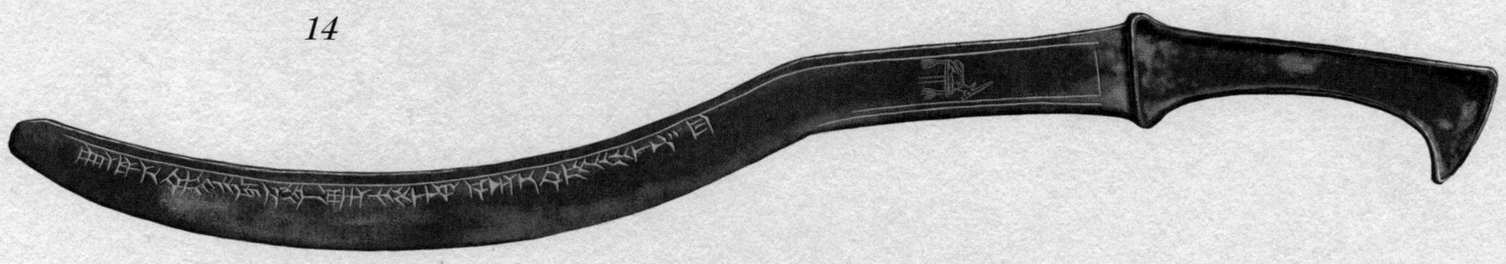

10: Lamassu

Around 883–859 BCE

Standing over 10 feet/3 meters high and 10 feet/3 meters long, this imposing stone sculpture, depicting a guardian figure known as a *lamassu*, is one of a pair that once stood outside the palace of Ashurnasirpal II in the Assyrian capital of Nimrud. The Mesopotamians believed demonic forces could bring death and destruction. Hybrid mythical creatures, like this winged bull with a man's head, were thought to have protective powers. The Assyrians glorified their kings over their gods, and their palaces became more prominent than their temples.

11: The Deluge Tablet

Seventh century BCE

This fragment of a clay tablet, roughly 6 by 5 inches/15 by 13 centimeters, recounts part of the *Epic of Gilgamesh*, the first great epic of world literature, which dates from around 2100 BCE, more than a thousand years before the *Iliad* or the *Odyssey*. It is written in Akkadian in an early form of writing called cuneiform. The tablet belonged to the Assyrian king Ashurbanipal, who had a library containing many thousands of cuneiform tablets.

Around 20,720 of them still survive today. This particular one, called the Deluge Tablet, is the most famous. It tells a story similar to the story of Noah and the great flood, but was written down four hundred years before the earliest versions of the Bible. Further discoveries at Ashurbanipal's library include letters, lists, legal texts, and scientific information. Ashurbanipal was the last of Assyria's great kings, reigning for more than forty years, from 668 to 627 BCE. His library was the first of its kind in the Middle East.

12: Royal cemetery, Ur: silver lyre

2600–2500 BCE

One of the graves excavated at Ur is known as the Great Death Pit because it contained the bodies of seventy-four attendants, mostly women, laid in rows. Whether these people were killed or went willingly to their deaths is unknown, but cups found near them suggest that they may have drunk poison. The six men were lying near the entrance with weapons. Near the women were three lyres, two of which, including the one shown here, were covered in sheet silver. Lyres like these were probably played at ritual ceremonies.

13: Royal cemetery, Ur: cuff beads

2600–2500 BCE

These beads probably formed elaborate cuffs on a long-sleeved garment. They were found on the female bodies in the royal tombs at Ur, along with many other adornments such as rings, pendants, headdresses, and earrings. A queen named Puabi was buried with fifty-two attendants and amazing adornments, as well as makeup, tweezers, and a tiny earwax spoon.

14: Sickle sword

1307–1275 BCE

The sickle sword was a symbol of power in Mesopotamia, and Mesopotamian art often depicts rulers and deities with these weapons. This bronze version, around 21 inches/ 54 centimeters long, belonged to the Assyrian king Adad-Nirari I, who ruled in the Late Bronze Age. An inscription in cuneiform, announcing his ownership, appears three times on the blade. Adad-Nirari probably used this sword in ceremonies rather than as an actual weapon.

The Ancient Levant

The ancient lands along the eastern coast of the Mediterranean Sea—where modern-day Syria, Lebanon, Israel, Palestine, and Jordan are located—are collectively known as the Levant. The area is one of the oldest continually inhabited regions of the world; ancient Syria and the region known in biblical literature as Canaan are located here.

The Canaanites had a sophisticated urban culture during the Middle and Late Bronze Age (2000–1200 BCE). They developed an early alphabet, from which Phoenician and other scripts derived. The Phoenicians, the greatest seafarers of the ancient world, were an Iron Age people who built on the traditions of the Canaanites. They were centered in what is now Lebanon, and their name derives from the purple-red dye used in their textile industry. They were renowned for their quality craftsmanship and were active traders.

Farther south, from around 1200 BCE, in the Late Bronze Age, the Israelites emerged. Their language, Hebrew, is closely related to Phoenician and other Canaanite languages. Their societies formed the foundations of the early Jewish kingdoms.

At times, large areas of the Levant were under the control of foreign powers, notably the Egyptians, the Assyrians, the Babylonians, and the Persians. Alexander the Great conquered the Levant in 332 BCE, and it later became part of the Roman Empire. It was under Roman occupation when Jesus is said to have been born, in the region known as Judea.

Key to plate

15: **Copper scepter**
4500–3500 BCE
This scepter is one of 442 objects discovered hidden in a cave in the Judean Desert near the Dead Sea. It is likely that the objects were sacred treasures from a nearby shrine, buried hurriedly for protection. Copper objects from the hoard, including this scepter, form the earliest known examples of the lost-wax casting process, in which a wax model is surrounded by a mold, the wax is melted, and molten metal is poured in to take its place.

16: **Ivory panel**
Ninth to eighth century BCE
This ivory panel is one of a nearly identical pair from the ancient Assyrian capital, Nimrud. The panels would have once been parts of a royal chair or throne. Phoenician-carved ivory and other craftwork was highly prized by the Assyrians. This panel was probably made in the Levant and came to Assyria as tribute or a spoil of war. It is

decorated in an Egyptian style, with lilies and papyrus plants. Originally it would have been lavishly coated in gold leaf and inlaid with semiprecious stones.

17: **Gold pendant**
1750–1550 BCE
This gold pendant depicts a Canaanite fertility goddess. It was found in Tell el-Ajjul, Gaza, which is thought to be the site of the ancient Canaanite city of Sharuhen. Around 2000 BCE, the Canaanites gradually moved southwest, into the Egyptian delta. By 1700 BCE, they had seized control of Egypt and established a dynasty that lasted until 1470 BCE.

18: **Statue of Idrimi**
Sixteenth century BCE
Idrimi was a king of the ancient Syrian city-state of Alalakh. This stone statue of him is covered in inscriptions recounting how his family fled their homeland, how he lived among Canaanite nomads, and how he then rallied an army around himself and

fought his way through ancient Syria to become king of Alalakh, which he ruled for thirty years.

19: **The Great Isaiah Scroll**
Around 125 BCE
In 1947, seven ancient scrolls were discovered by a Bedouin shepherd boy in a cave in the Judean Desert. Extensive searches of the area uncovered 1,400 documents made of animal skin, papyrus, and, in some cases, copper. Together they are known as the Dead Sea Scrolls, and they cover nearly all of the Hebrew Bible, as well as other non-biblical books. The Great Isaiah Scroll, shown here, is the best-preserved document and also the largest, measuring 24 feet/7.34 meters when unrolled. It contains all sixty-six chapters of the biblical Book of Isaiah and is written in Hebrew in fifty-four columns. The scrolls are remarkable since they predate any other written versions of the Hebrew Bible by more than one thousand years.

15

16

17

18

19

Ancient Persia

At its height, the Persian Empire was the largest yet seen in the ancient world. It extended from Anatolia and Egypt east to northern India and central Asia. Founded by Cyrus the Great, who reigned from 559 to 530 BCE and was from the clan of Achaemenes, it is also known as the Achaemenid Empire.

In the sixth century BCE, Cyrus united the Iranian tribes living in the region southeast of Babylon, known as Persia. He led them on a series of campaigns, conquering the empire of the Medes, the Anatolian kingdom of Lydia, and the Greek cities of Asia Minor. In 539 BCE, his soldiers defeated the Babylonian army, but Cyrus did not take Babylon by force. He presented himself as a traditional Mesopotamian monarch, more respectful of the people's traditions than their unpopular king, Nabonidus. The city gates were opened to him, and Babylon became part of the Persian Empire. Egypt was later added to the empire by Cyrus's son, Cambyses II.

The third Achaemenid king, Darius the Great, who reigned from 522 to 486 BCE, is credited with stabilizing the Persian Empire and expanding it to its greatest extent. He introduced an efficient system of regional governors and an impressive network of roads. He displayed his power through two major building projects: a new capital, Persepolis, in his Persian homeland, and a royal palace complex at Susa.

The Persian Empire lasted just over two centuries. Its rulers managed to suppress revolts in Egypt, but ultimately they could not hold back the Greeks. In 330 BCE, Alexander the Great and his men fought their way across the Persian provinces. Although they faced great resistance, they succeeded in gaining the empire.

Key to plate

---

20 (opposite page): **Frieze of archers**
Around 510 BCE
The colorful glazed bricks that make up this stunning frieze were discovered during excavations at the site of Darius the Great's palace at Susa. Thousands more glazed bricks have been found on the site, suggesting that processions of archers may have covered hundreds of meters of the exterior palace walls.

The archers may represent Darius's elite group of soldiers, called the Immortals by the Greek historian Herodotus. They were said to always number 10,000 men; if one died, he was immediately replaced, giving the impression of immortality. Alternatively, the archers may be idealized images of Persian men. They wear long, decorative Persian robes, belted at the waist, and laced ankle boots. Their spears, held upright, have a rounded weight at the lower end for counterbalance. This weight earned Persian soldiers fighting Alexander the Great the nickname "Apple Bearers."

This frieze was probably inspired by the Processional Way in Babylon, a stone- and brick-paved avenue that ran from the city's temples to its royal palaces. Centuries after the Persian Empire, glazed-brick decoration would become a prominent feature of Islamic architecture.

Early Islam

The faith of Islam was established by the prophet Muhammad in the seventh century CE. It began in Arabia and spread rapidly across the Middle East through a series of military conquests. Following the death of the prophet Muhammad in 632 CE, the Muslim community was led by a caliph (meaning "successor"), and the growing Islamic empire under his command became known as the caliphate.

In the eighth to tenth centuries CE, the caliphate stretched from central Asia to Spain. Islam was more than a religion; it was a way of life, and it fostered a distinct culture and style of art and architecture. Artifacts from the early Islamic period show how Islamic art emerged from a blend of Iranian and classical influences.

The caliphate experienced a golden age during the Abbasid Dynasty. Baghdad was established as the capital city in 762 CE and became a prosperous center of culture and commerce, earning a reputation as the richest city in the world. For a brief interlude in the ninth century CE, the caliphs used the city of Samarra as their capital. Although it was abandoned less than sixty years later, it is of major archaeological interest since virtually nothing remains of the Abbasid period in Baghdad, which was sacked and destroyed by the Mongols in 1258 CE. The Mongols killed the caliph, and their invasion ended the Abbasid Dynasty. Although the Islamic faith and culture continued to spread, the Arab-Muslim empire was at an end.

Key to plate

21: Woven tapestry fragment
Mid-eighth century CE
This woolen tapestry is from the Umayyad period (661–750 CE), the first Islamic dynasty. Art from this time was still influenced by pre-Islamic traditions and techniques. Here, the repeat rosette pattern can be traced to Sasanian art. The Sasanian Dynasty followed the ancient Zoroastrian religion and controlled Iran from 224 to 642 CE. The abstract ornamentation of the Sasanians was the precursor to the geometric and vegetal (plant-shaped) patterns of Islamic art. The red border on this tapestry suggests that it was used as a floor covering. The manufacture and trade of textiles flourished in early Islamic society. Often made of luxury materials, textiles were symbols of status.

22: Wall painting fragments
Ninth century CE
The city of Samarra was built in 836 CE, 70 miles/110 kilometers north of Baghdad, as a new capital for the Islamic empire. Its name is a shortening of the Arabic for "he who sees it is delighted," and its vast palaces and barracks were intended to dazzle visitors. These paintings, however, were hidden from view in the harem quarters, where the women of the court lived, and were intended only for the eyes of the caliph and those close to him.

The faces most likely depict the female slaves who lived and worked there. They would have been skilled poets, musicians, dancers, and singers, and they lived alongside the caliph's wives. Flecks of gold in the paintings suggest that they were originally more lavish. These fragments provide examples of the early depiction of figures in Islamic art.

23: Earthenware bowl
Eleventh century CE
Arabic is the language in which the Qur'an is said to have been revealed to Muhammad and is therefore held in great esteem in Islamic culture. The art of writing Arabic is also highly prized, and from early in the Islamic era, a sophisticated calligraphy developed. This bowl from Nishapur, in northeastern Iran, features the oldest calligraphic form of Arabic, known as Kufic script. The words translate as "Blessing, prosperity, well-being, and happiness." Inscriptions are a common feature on early Islamic pottery. They never state historical facts but often give advice on how to lead a good life.

Gallery 6

Oceania

Indigenous Australians
Melanesia
Polynesia
The Māori

Indigenous Australians

The Aboriginal people and the Torres Strait Islanders are the indigenous people of Australia, and their cultures are among the oldest in the world. Aboriginal people settled in mainland Australia more than 50,000 years ago. The world's first known seafarers, they arrived by boat from Asia. The Torres Strait Islanders are of Melanesian descent. They arrived in the Torres Strait area when it was still a land bridge linking Australia to New Guinea. Between 15,000 and 8,000 years ago, the sea level rose, leaving only the Torres Strait Islands above water.

Over the millennia, there has been frequent contact between Torres Strait Islanders and the Aboriginal people. They share a deep spiritual connection with their natural environment and strong traditions of storytelling, ceremonies, and visual arts, but their cultures are distinct and the Torres Strait Islanders' traditions are more closely related to the Papuan culture of New Guinea.

By 20,000 years ago, Aboriginal people had spread across the whole of mainland Australia and into Tasmania. Different territorial groups adapted to contrasting climates and terrains and developed their own languages. They were traditionally hunter-gatherers and lived in small, nomadic groups, but would come together for ceremonies at sacred sites. The Aboriginal people held in common a worldview, known as the Dreaming, which links the present and the future to a mythical beginning. Art has always been an important medium for expressing the Dreaming, and Aboriginal people would decorate any available surfaces, from rocks and sand to their own bodies and pieces of bark.

The arrival of British colonists from 1788 CE decimated the Aboriginal population through violence, repression, and exposure to new diseases. The Torres Strait Islander population also declined. Aboriginal and Torres Strait Islander numbers have since recovered, and today there are over 500,000 Aboriginal people and 50,000 Torres Strait Islanders living in Australia. Their cultures are very much alive, cherished, and continuing to evolve.

--- *Key to plate* ---

1 (opposite page): **Rock painting**
500–1500 CE
Rock art in Australia dates back at least 25,000 years, and there are more than 125,000 rock art sites. The art styles differ over time and place, but nearly all the paintings have spiritual meanings. Images of creatures and humans act as intermediaries between the everyday world and the supernatural. Caves and cliff faces bearing rock art are sacred places, with successive generations of artists tasked with touching up the artwork so its spiritual power does not diminish.

This rock painting dates from the Freshwater Period (from 500 CE or later) and is at Ubirr, in Kakadu National Park, in northern Australia. It shows a hunter, painted in red ochre, holding spears and a goose-wing fan for fanning a fire. Over his shoulder is a bag for carrying food. This hunter is one of many lively figures shown dancing, running, or fighting. They are said to be spirit people, called *mimi*, who live in the rock face.

2: **Torres Strait Islander mask**
Nineteenth century CE
Torres Strait Islanders have a rich tradition of carving and creating elaborate masks and headdresses. These are worn during ceremonies and rituals as part of an ongoing relationship with the spirit world. This mask is carved in wood, decorated with shell and natural pigments, and topped with human hair. Many ritual objects were destroyed when Christian missionaries arrived on the islands.

2

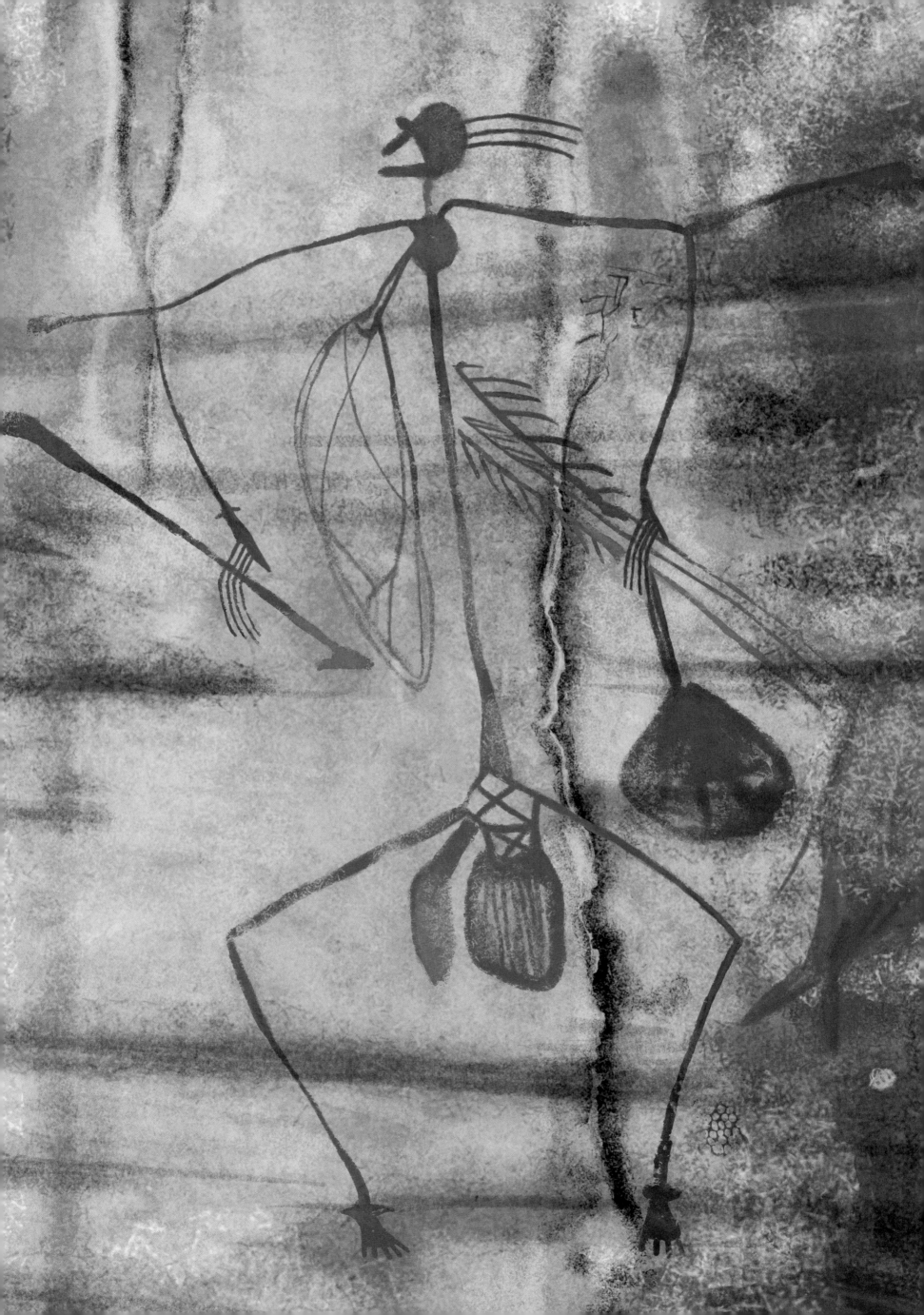

Melanesia

Stretching in an arc to the northeast of Australia, in the western Pacific Ocean, are the islands of Melanesia. They include the island of New Guinea, the Solomon Islands, Vanuatu, New Caledonia, and Fiji. People have lived on New Guinea for more than 40,000 years and on the Solomon Islands for more than 30,000 years. From around 1500 BCE, seafaring settlers, originally from Southeast Asia, spread through Melanesia and later Polynesia, bringing with them a culture known as Lapita.

Across the islands of Melanesia, people have traditionally lived in small communities based on kinship, although there were also larger villages, especially in coastal regions. Inter-island communities were often linked by trade networks, which could involve canoe voyages over long distances. Shell beads and dolphin teeth were among the valuable exchange items, and shells or feathers were used as currency in some areas. People kept pigs, grew root crops, went hunting and fishing, and performed regular rituals. Religion was part of everyday life, through a belief in ghosts and spirits as invisible beings on earth. Magic and spells were used to encourage a good harvest or a successful hunting trip.

Beginning in the seventeenth century CE, Melanesia came under colonial influences, which disrupted local networks and traditions. In the late nineteenth century CE, Christianity was introduced, causing significant cultural changes. Some areas, especially in the highlands of New Guinea, remained unaffected by outside influences until the twentieth century. Despite this, many Melanesian cultural traditions continued in these communities, and others are being revived.

Key to plate

3: Ambum stone
Around 1500 BCE
Sculpted stone items from the island of New Guinea are among the earliest known Pacific works of art. Many are shaped as animals and humans, and this figure, known as the Ambum stone, may well represent a type of spiny anteater called an echidna. It is one of the most detailed early New Guinean rock sculptures discovered. The purpose of these objects is unknown, but the time and care taken to make them — the hard rock would have taken weeks to shape with stone tools — suggest that they were used in rituals.

4: Lapita pottery
1000 BCE
These pottery pieces belong to the Lapita culture. Lapita pottery is distinctive for its geometric patterns. On this example, found in the Santa Cruz Islands, in the southeastern Solomon Islands, a symmetrical human face is clearly visible amid the decoration. The Lapita culture reached as far as Tonga and Samoa, in Polynesia, and its patterns are echoed in modern Polynesian design.

5: Chubwan mask
Fifteenth to seventeenth century CE
This mask from the island of Pentecost, in the Vanuatu island group, was carved from hardwood using a stone tool or a clam shell, then sanded down using the rough skin of a ray or a shark. The mask's exact function is unknown, but most likely it was worn at ritual events, perhaps to scare off the spirits of the dead. Its deep-set eyes and skillfully exaggerated features seem intended to intimidate.

6: Paddle
Nineteenth to early twentieth century CE
This beautifully decorated paddle comes from Bougainville Island, northwest of the Solomon Islands. The islanders made special canoes for head-hunting raids. By acquiring human heads, a warrior could increase his status in the community. The stylized figures on this paddle depict powerful spirits, known as *kokorra*. The paddle may have been intended to give spiritual protection, or it may have been purely ceremonial. The practice of head-hunting had ended by the early twentieth century.

7: Malangan funerary carving
Nineteenth to early twentieth century CE
This 52-inch-/133-centimeter-tall wooden figure is an early surviving example of *malangan* carving from New Ireland, an island east of New Guinea. These figures are used in a cycle of rituals, known as *malangan*, which includes ceremonies for nearly every stage of life. The most detailed and impressive carvings are made for funerary rites. The figures celebrate the life of the deceased, and animal and human figures may represent myths or be spiritually linked to particular clans. After they have been used, *malangan* carvings are destroyed, abandoned, or sold outside the island.

Polynesia

The islands of Polynesia form a triangle, with Rapa Nui (Easter Island), Hawai'i, and Aotearoa (New Zealand) marking its three corners. Lapita settlers, known for their geometrically patterned pottery, reached Fiji, Tonga, and Samoa by around 1000 BCE. Over the next thousand years, Lapita pottery disappeared and new, distinct Polynesian cultures emerged.

Around 100 BCE to 200 CE, Polynesian people expanded eastward to islands including what we now call the Marquesas, the Cook Islands, and the Society Islands. It took several hundred years for them to reach the more remote islands, with Hawai'i being settled around 500 CE, Rapa Nui around 600 CE, and a permanent settlement being established on Aotearoa (New Zealand) around 1250 to 1300 CE.

The Polynesians were excellent seafarers. Their expert navigation, which relied on the stars, the flight paths of migratory birds, and the patterns of sea currents and wind, meant they were able to travel huge distances. In their wooden canoes, they carried everything they needed to survive, including root crops, plant seedlings, Polynesian rats and dogs (an important food source), weapons, and tools. Their strong sense of cultural identity was conserved over the centuries and across vast stretches of ocean. Before European contact, most Polynesians lived in small family groups, cultivating plantations and fishing. Most islands were divided into chiefdoms, with the chiefs' families making up an aristocracy.

Polynesian people revered many gods and celebrated ancestral heroes. Daily life and rituals were governed by strict protocols, with a strong sense of what was sacred, or tapu. Tasks were often gendered, with men making most of the wooden or stone objects and women making bark cloth, baskets, and feathered cloaks. The Polynesian islands changed radically after colonization and with the arrival of Christianity, yet Polynesian identities remain strong and many ancient practices continue today.

Key to plate

8: Hoa Hakananai'a, Rapa Nui
Around 1000 CE

Forming the most isolated corner of the Polynesian triangle, Rapa Nui, or Easter Island, is 1,200 miles/1,900 kilometers from the nearest inhabited island; that Polynesian setters reached it is testament to their navigation expertise. Beyond the initial settlement, there is no evidence of continuing contact with other islands.

The population of Rapa Nui grew to around 15,000, and over a period of several hundred years, they produced hundreds of astonishing stone statues known as *moai*. The *moai* are massive. This one towers over a human at 9 feet/2.7 meters, but others are more than 33 feet/10 meters tall. They were chipped out of rock using stone tools, then transported considerable distances to stand in lines along the coast. They were positioned on specially constructed stone platforms with their backs to the sea, facing a ceremonial courtyard area. Each statue is a unique stone being, portraying an ancestral chief who would watch over the living and offer protection.

The immense effort required to create and transport the *moai* suggests that they were of utmost importance to life on Rapa Nui, and yet they ceased to be constructed around 1600 CE. After centuries of habitation, there was a natural decline in the environment of the island, and many seabirds—a staple food—had moved away. In response to their changing environment, the islanders adopted a new religious tradition: the cult of the birdman. Each year they competed to be the first to bring back an unbroken egg from a rocky islet. The winner became the birdman for a year, living alone and gaining sacred powers.

This *moai*, known as Hoa Hakananai'a (loosely meaning "hidden friend"), played a part in the new cult too. It was moved to a shelter, and its reverse was carved and brightly painted with birdman symbols. In 1868, the *moai* was given to officers of a British ship. By then, the population of the island had plummeted to several hundred people. The islanders had survived and adapted to ecological changes, but contact with Europeans from the early eighteenth century had brought devastating diseases, civil unrest, and the loss of many people to the slave trade. The population of Rapa Nui has since recovered and now numbers over five thousand, 60 percent of whom are native islanders.

8

_9:_ A'a figure, Austral Islands

Eighteenth to early nineteenth century CE
Some of the finest wood carvings in
Polynesia were done in the Cook and
Austral Islands. This carving, from the
Austral island of Rurutu, is thought to
represent the local deity, A'a, in the act
of creating people. Thirty unique little
figures appear to be emerging from all
over the deity. The carving is hollow,
with a removable lid, and once held
many more little figures.

_10:_ 'Akau tau, Tonga

Eighteenth century AD
This finely decorated 'akau tau, or war
club, is from Tonga and was possibly
taken to England by the explorer
Captain James Cook. The detailed
geometric designs, characteristic of
Tongan war clubs, are reminiscent of
the Lapita patterns made by Tongan
ancestors. The handle is more roughly

carved to give a firm grip, while the
finer decorations may have been
incised with a shark's tooth. Clubs
like these often depict tiny figures,
animals, birds, and plants, and appear
to tell stories. They were revered as
weapons and as sacred objects, with
names and lives of their own.

_11:_ Head of a staff god, Rarotonga

Eighteenth to early nineteenth century CE
In Polynesia, figures of gods, or _atua_,
carved in wood, were important
sacred objects, looked after by priests.
This carving, from Rarotonga, in the
Cook Islands, would have formed the
top end of a type of figure known as a
staff god, which would have stood 29
feet/6 meters high. When Christian
missionaries arrived in the late
eighteenth century CE, they rejected
the _atua_. Many Rarotongan islanders
then gave up their god sculptures and

burned their religious buildings. The left
side of this carving has been violently
damaged, including multiple stab marks
in the eye, perhaps the result of an
attempt to destroy its power.

_12:_ Palāhega, Niue

Eighteenth or nineteenth century CE
Throughout Polynesia, the feathers of
particular birds were used for the most
prestigious items. The bright plumage
of various small parrots was valued for
cloaks, girdles, helmets, headdresses,
and god figures. The tail feathers of
the tropic bird were also gathered and
used in large quantities, even though
each bird has just two of these elegant
long quills. This headdress, or _palāhega_,
is from Niue. Tropic-bird tail feathers
protrude from its shaft, which is
wrapped in red and blue feathers and
bound with thinly braided human hair.
Human hair was believed to contain a

OCEANIA

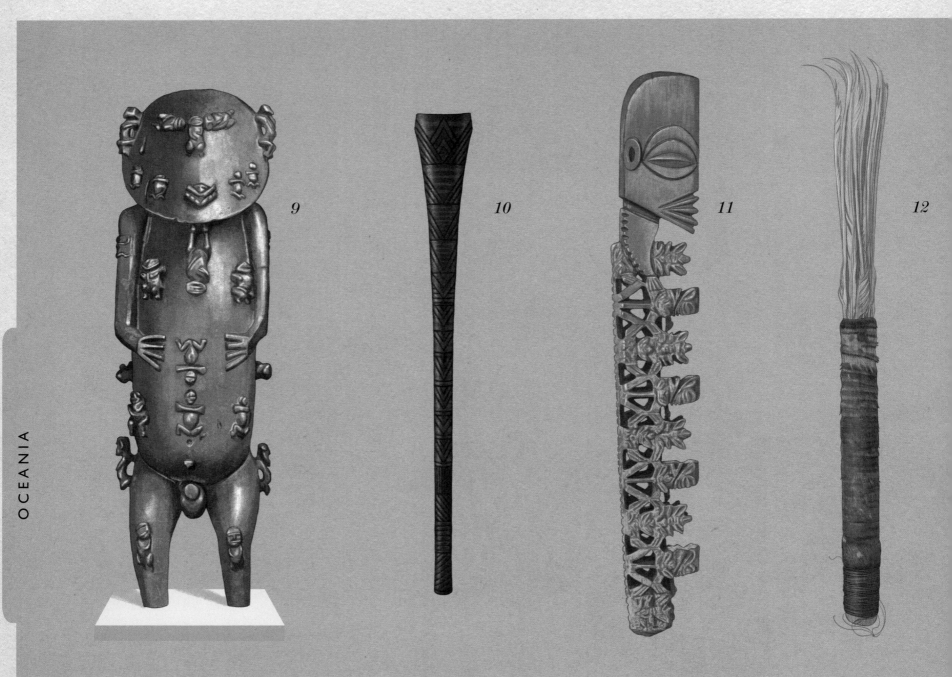

9 10 11 12

person's *mana* (prestige or power) and was used in items of high status. This beautiful *palāhega* (pronounced *pa-lar-heng-a*) was worn at the back of the head, with its long feathers projecting to the sky.

13: *Tanoa fai'ava*, Samoa
Late eighteenth to early nineteenth century CE

Kava is a ceremonial drink, made from the roots of the pepper bush, that numbs the tongue and relaxes the body. It would be offered as a welcome drink to strangers and passed around during important meetings. This *tanoa fai'ava,* or kava bowl, is an early example from Samoa. Early Samoan kava bowls like this one have four legs, while more recent examples have many more. Kava ceremonies still take place in Polynesian communities.

14: *Hakakai*, Marquesas Islands
Early nineteenth century CE

These exquisitely carved *hakakai,* or ivory ear ornaments, come from the Marquesas Islands, now part of modern French Polynesia. *Hakakai* were worn by both men and women. The most prestigious *hakakai* were made of whalebone, which was extremely rare and valuable, since before European contact it was obtained only from stranded whales. Whalebone *hakakai* became more common in the nineteenth century, when European and American whalers brought more of the precious material to the islands. This finely crafted pair dates from that era.

15: *Kapa*, Hawai'i
Eighteenth century CE

Bark cloth was made in most parts of Polynesia and was used for both sacred and practical purposes. It is still made today. As well as being used for clothing, bedding, and room dividers, it also marked boundaries between the realms of living humans and ancestors, keeping people safe from *tapu,* highly sacred areas or objects, and from high-ranking people's *mana.* It could be laid on the ground for important people to walk on, or wrapped around them to contain their *mana.* It was also wrapped around some of the most potent god figures. Bark cloth was made from the inner bark of certain trees, soaked and beaten with a mallet upon an anvil into lengths of pliable cloth, then pasted or felted together and decorated with plant dyes.

This piece of bark cloth is from Hawai'i, where it is called *kapa.* Hawaiian *kapa* is intricately decorated and scented.

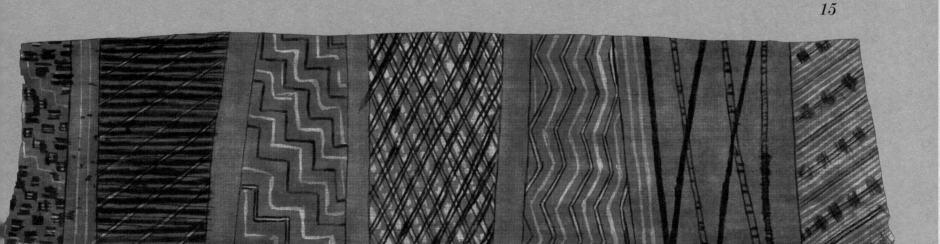

13

14

15

The Māori

Māori are the descendants of the Polynesians who settled in Aotearoa (New Zealand) around 1250 to 1300 CE. *Aotearoa* means "land of the long white cloud" and is thought to describe how the North Island first appeared to Polynesian explorers. New Zealand's two large islands have a colder climate and very different flora and fauna from the small tropical islands the settlers had left behind, but the Māori adapted to their new environment. Plants, animals, birds, and seafood were gathered and hunted, and the *kūmara,* or Polynesian sweet potato, was cultivated in warmer areas of the country as an important food source.

Māori society divided itself into different *iwi* (tribes), each tracing its roots to one of the settlers' canoes. There was a strict hierarchy, based on ancestry, and a sharp distinction between the aristocrats and the commoners. Wars often broke out between and even within *iwi*. Māori warriors were cunning in their battle strategies and use of fortifications. Fortified villages, known as *pā,* were often built on hills for strategic advantage, and impressive trenches and ramparts—some dating from as late as the mid-nineteenth century CE—can still be seen in the New Zealand landscape.

Art and religion were strongly connected in Māori culture. Expert wood-carvers and tattoo artists traditionally shared the title *tohunga* with priests, and through their careful designs they were thought to give supernatural powers to everyday objects. The most precious material was a hard jade-like stone, *pounamu.* Māori women were also expert weavers and created beautiful mats and ceremonial cloaks.

Metal tools reached New Zealand through contact with Europeans from the seventeenth century CE onward. These tools enabled Māori carvings to become increasingly detailed and elaborate. Māori culture, craftsmanship, and a strong sense of identity still thrive today. Both traditional and contemporary art forms are practiced by the Māori and hold great cultural significance.

Key to plate

16: Adze blade
1500–1820 CE
Adzes were a common hand tool in Stone Age cultures. The shape of this blade matches ones made by the earliest settlers in New Zealand and is similar to eastern Polynesian examples. Blades were bound by fiber to wooden handles, then used to cut and carve wood and to hollow out canoes. This blade, made of *pounamu,* is surprisingly large, at 17 inches/44 centimeters long, and was probably for ceremonial use by a high-status person, maybe a chief.

17: Hand club
Late eighteenth to nineteenth century CE
Traditionally, the Māori fought using spears and clubs. Warriors carried *patu,* short clubs, in their belts and used them to give their enemies a final blow to the head. The clubs were made of wood, bone, or stone, with a hole in the handle for attaching a wrist cord. This club is a particularly fine example. Made of *pounamu* and carved with a head on the handle, it would have been a prized possession.

18: Hei tiki
1600–1850 CE
This pendant, carved in *pounamu,* shows a human-like figure known as a *hei tiki.* The origins of *hei tiki* are unknown, but their curious shape has long been a symbol of fertility and womanhood, perhaps representing an important female ancestor or an unborn child. Another theory is that it is a representation of Tiki, the first man. Pendants such as this one have long been treasured and passed from one generation to the next.

19: Fishhook
1750–1850 CE
Fishing was of great importance to the Māori. Not only did fish form a major part of their diet, but they were also thought of as descendants of Tangaroa, god of the sea, and fishing was seen as a *tapu,* or sacred, activity. According to legend, the whole of New Zealand's North Island was a great fish raised out of the sea on the hero Maui's fishhook. This *pounamu* fishhook is ornamental, to be worn as a pendant or a brooch, probably as a representation of Maui's hook.

20: Prow from a war canoe
Eighteenth century CE
Māori carving was imbued with sacred significance. The sinuous, eel-like decorations on this prow, known as *manaia,* are part animal, part human, and are thought to represent the spiritual side of life. The prow is from New Zealand's Northland and would have decorated the front of a war canoe. Particular care was taken when crafting a war canoe. It was a work of art, an efficient mode of transport, and a display of power. Often more than 66 feet/20 meters long, decorated with paint and feathers and carrying up to 140 tattooed warriors, it was designed to both impress and intimidate.

Library

Indexes
Curators
Image Credits

General Index

Index of Museums and Collections

The artifacts displayed in *Historium* come from all over the world. Most are in museums, where they may be viewed by the public when on display. *

* While many of the objects in *Historium* are held in museum collections, there is no guarantee that objects will be on display at any given time.

Curators

Richard Wilkinson is a self-taught illustrator living and working in Brighton, England. His work has appeared in *New Scientist*, *Intelligent Life*, and *Time*.

Jo Nelson studied modern and medieval languages at Cambridge University, England. She has been researching and writing nonfiction books for fifteen years.

Image Credits

Africa

Item 1, left (also p. 4): Steven J H Walker. Item 2 (also p. 4): Image courtesy of Prof. Christopher Henshilwood, University of Bergen, Norway. Items 3, 6 (also p. 5): Images courtesy of Iziko Museums of South Africa. Items 4 (also front cover & p. 5), 5 (scepter also on front cover): Images courtesy of the University of Pretoria Museums, Mapungubwe Collection. Item 8: Artist's drawing of equestrian figure, Inland Niger Delta Style, Mali, 13th–15th century, ceramic, 70.5 × 15.2 × 45.7 cm. (27¾ × 6 × 18 in.), Museum purchase, 86-12-2, National Museum of African Art, Smithsonian Institution, Washington, DC. Item 9 (also pp. 5, 6 & back cover): Illustration based on photograph by Marie-Lan Nguyen. Items 12 (also p. 5), 14, 15 (also p. 7), 16 (also p. 4), 26 (also p. xii), 28: © 2015 Images copyright The Metropolitan Museum of Art/Art Resource/Scala, Florence. Item 20 (also p. 4): Illustration based on photograph by Philip Pikart.

America

Item 1 (also pp. 4, 23 & front cover): CONACULTA-INAH-MEX. Reproduction authorized by National Institute of Anthropology and History, Mexico. Item 2 (also p. 4 & front cover): CONACULTA-INAH-MEX. Reproduction authorized by National Institute of Anthropology and History, Mexico. Item 3: © 2015 Kimbell Art Museum, Fort Worth, Texas/Art Resource, NY/Scala, Florence. Items 4, 5, 17: © 2015 Images copyright The Metropolitan Museum of Art/Art Resource/Scala, Florence. Item 6 (also p. 5 & cover): CONACULTA-INAH-MEX. Reproduction authorized by National Institute of Anthropology and History, Mexico. Item 8: CONACULTA-INAH-MEX. Reproduction authorized by National Institute of Anthropology and History, Mexico. Item 9 (also p. 22 & front cover): CONACULTA-INAH-MEX. Reproduction authorized by National Institute of Anthropology and History, Mexico. Item 11: Courtesy of Ohio History Connection (A125/000021). Item 12 (also back cover): Courtesy of the Ohio History Connection (A 3874/000001) (loan). Item 13 (also p. 5 & back cover): Courtesy of Ohio History Connection (A0283/000294). Item 15 (also p. 5): National Museum of the American Indian, Smithsonian Institution (5/2109), photo by NMAI Photo Services. Item 16: National Museum of the American Indian, Smithsonian Institution (5/1364), photo by Ernest Amoroso.

Asia

Item 2 (also p. 4): National Museum – New Delhi Collection, acc no: 5721/195. Item 4: National Museum – New Delhi Collection, acc no: 83.126. Items 6, 10, 11, 15, 17: © 2015 Images copyright The Metropolitan Museum of Art/Art Resource/Scala, Florence. Item 7: National Museum – New Delhi Collection, acc no: 47.20. Item 8 (also p. 5 & front cover): Xuzhou Museum. Item 9 (also p. 36): Freer Gallery of Art, Smithsonian Institution, Washington, DC: Gift of Charles Lang Freer, F1915.103a-b. Item 12 (also p. 4): Illustration based on photograph by Yan Li. Item 13: Arthur M. Sackler Gallery, Smithsonian Institution, Washington, DC: Gift of Arthur M Sackler, S1987.655. Item 18 (also back cover): Tokyo National Museum. Item 19 (also p. 5): photograph provided by Nara National Museum, the Collection of Nara National Museum. Item 20 (also pp. 2 & 5): Gyeongju National Museum of Korea, Gold Crown from the North Mound of Hwangnamdaechong Tomb, Hwangbuk No. 1, Gyeongju. Item 21: Gyeongju National Museum of Korea, House-shaped Funeral Urn (Bukgun-dong), Sinsu No.1121, Gyeongju. Item 22: Gyeongju National Museum of Korea, Iron chanfron – iron horse armor/Sara-ri Tomb No. 65, Gyeongju. Item 23 (also p. 37): National Museum of Korea, Gilt-bronze Maitreya in Meditation (National Treasure No. 83).

Europe

Items 2, 4: Illustrations based on photographs by Xuan Che. Item 5 (also p. 5): photograph © The British Library Board, Cotton Nero D IV f137v. Items 7 (also p. 50), 8, 10 (also p. 4), 14, 22: © 2015 Images copyright The Metropolitan Museum of Art/Art Resource/Scala, Florence. Item 11: Khan Academy. Item 15: Photo © Vatican Museum; all rights reserved; original statue in the collection of Vatican Museums; reproduced with permission of the Vatican Museums. Item 19: With permission of the Ministry of Cultural Heritage and Tourism – Superintendency for the Archaeological Heritage of Naples and Pompeii. Item 23: Illustration based on photograph by Carole Raddato. Artifact represented with permission of the Ministry of Cultural Heritage and Tourism – Superintendency for the Archaeological Heritage of Naples and Pompeii. Items 25, 26: National Museum of Denmark.

The Middle East

Items 2, 6, 14, 21 (also p. 5), 23 (also p. 5): © 2015 Images copyright The Metropolitan Museum of Art/Art Resource/Scala, Florence. Item 7: Illustration after D. 019208: Male Statue, Tell Asmar (A12332); courtesy of the Oriental Institute of the University of Chicago. Items 15 & 19: (also pp. 4 & 5): Images © The Israel Museum, Jerusalem. Item 20 (also p. 5): Based on photograph by Mohammed Shamma.

Oceania

Item 1 (also p. 5): Rock Art illustrated and reproduced with kind permission of the traditional owners from the East Alligator Region, Kakadu National Park. Item 2: Unknown Artist, Torres Strait Islands, Queensland, Mawa mask 19th century, wood, shell, resin, human, hair, fiber string, white string, 42 × 22 × 13 cm. (12½ × 8 ¾ × 5 in.), National Gallery of Australia, Canberra, purchased 2006. Item 3: Ambum Valley, Western Highlands, Papua New Guinea, the Ambum stone 3500–6000 years ago, greywacke stone, 20 × 7.5 × 14 cm. (7 ⅞ × 3 × 5 ½ in.), National Gallery of Australia, Canberra, purchased 1977. Item 4 (also p. 4): Courtesy of the Anthropology Photographic Archive, Department of Anthropology, The University of Auckland. Item 5: Chubwan mask, Pentecost Island, Penama province, Vanuatu Melanesia, wood, patina, 24.0 × 14.5 × 11.5 cm. (9 ½ × 5 ¾ × 4½ in.), National Gallery of Australia, Canberra, Purchased 2011. Items 6, 7, 14: © 2015 Images copyright The Metropolitan Museum of Art/Art Resource/Scala, Florence. Item 10: 'akau-tau (club), 1700s, Tonga, maker unknown; gift of Lord St. Oswald, 1912; Te Papa (FE000339). Item 12: Based on photograph by Billie Lythberg with permission of Knut Rio. Item 13 (also p. 81): Tanoa fai'ava (kava bowl), 1800s, Samoa, maker unknown; gift of Mrs. Louisa Kronfeld, 1939; Te Papa (FE010512). Item 15: Kapa (tapa), 1770s, Hawaii, maker unknown. Gift of Dr. P. Adams, 1947; Te Papa (FE005246). Item 16: Toki poutangata (ceremonial nephrite adze blade), 1500–1820, New Zealand, maker unknown; Oldman Collection; gift of the New Zealand Government, 1992; Te Papa (OL000117). Item 18 (also p. 5 & 80): Hei tiki (pendant in human form), 1600–1850, maker unknown. Purchased 1972; Te Papa (ME012842). Item 19: Matau (fishhook), 1750–1850, New Zealand, maker unknown; Oldman Collection; gift of the New Zealand Government, 1992; Te Papa (OL000097).

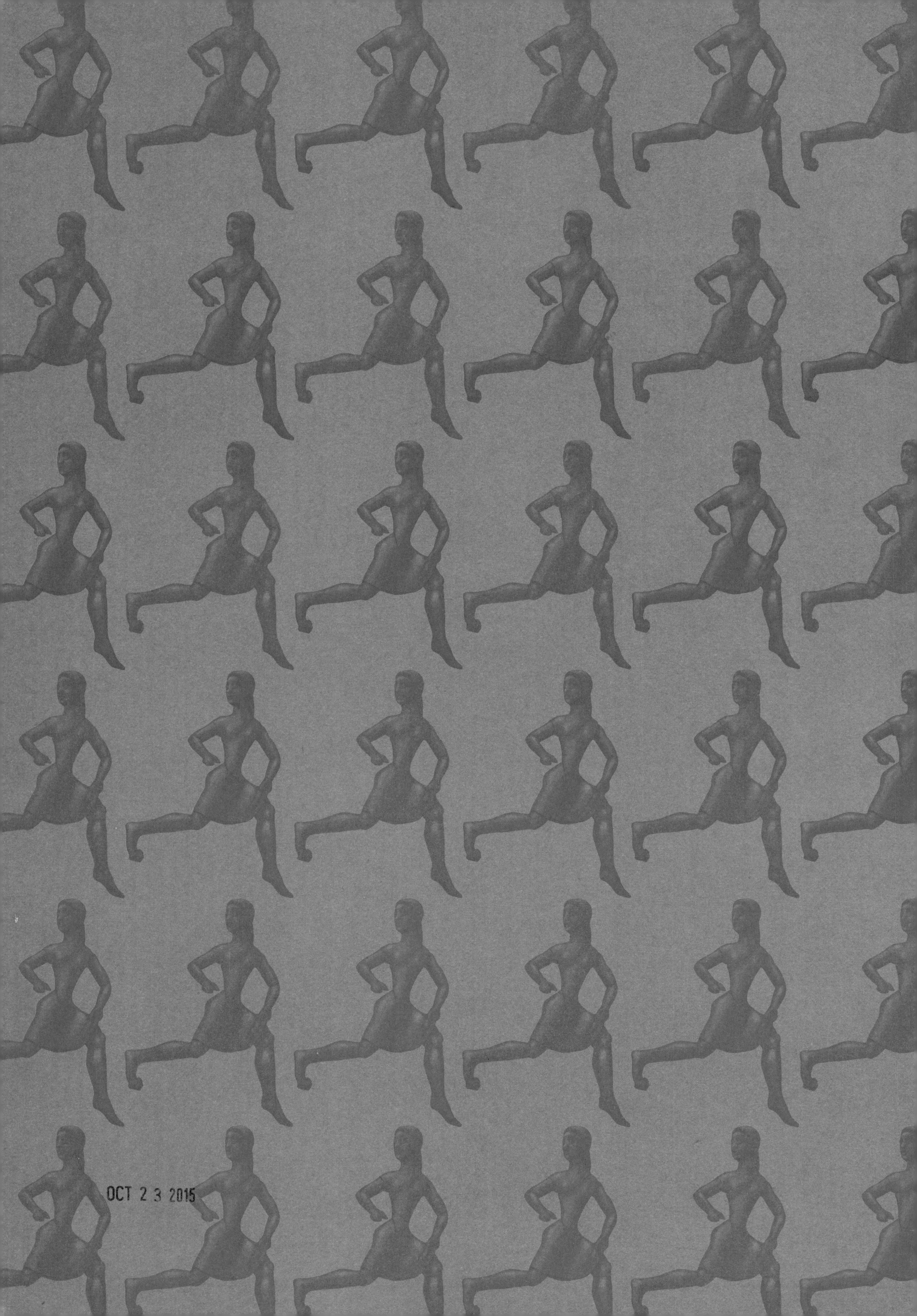